CW00336099

WITHDRAWN
FOR SALE

THE HEALTHY
CAT BOOK

Also by Alexandra Bastedo and Jeannie Kemnitzer and published
by Robson Books

Canine Care and Cuisine

THE HEALTHY CAT BOOK

FELINE CARE AND CUISINE

ALEXANDRA BASTEDO
and
JEANNIE KEMNITZER

Robson Books

First published in Great Britain in 1998 by Robson Books Ltd, Bolsover House, 5–6 Clipstone Street, London W1P 8LE

Copyright © 1998 Alexandra Bastedo

Copyright © 1998 Jeannie Kemnitzer for linking passages with researched literary quotes and recipes contained in Meaty Meals, Fish Fodder, Drink or Treat and Recipes for Ailing Cats sections

The right of Alexandra Bastedo and Jeannie Kemnitzer to be identified as authors of this work has been asserted by them in accordance with the Copyright, Designs and Patents Act 1988

British Library Cataloguing in Publication Data
A catalogue record for this title is available from the British Library

ISBN 1 86105 178 6

Illustrations © Pollyanna Pickering

Disclaimer: The health suggestions in this book are not meant in any way to replace sound professional advice. The authors and publisher shall have neither liability nor responsibility for any cat or person with respect to any illness, loss or damage caused, or alleged to be caused, directly or indirectly, by the information contained in this book.

Typeset in 10.5/14pt Stone Serif by Columns Design Ltd., Reading.
Printed in Great Britain by St Edmundsbury Press, Bury St Edmunds, Suffolk

CONTENTS

PREFACE

Many aspects of pet care have changed over the last 10 years or so. Some of the developments in human medicine have reached the veterinary profession. We have better diagnostic techniques, a vast array of modern medicines, complete ranges of scientifically formulated foods and the latest computer aided technology to hand. Sadly, in some ways, the art of veterinary medicine has become more business orientated and scientific with a move away from the very personal, hands-on level at which it was once practised.

Not surprisingly, behind the scenes, interest in complementary or alternative veterinary medicine has been growing steadily, keeping pace with technology. This has not only been driven by pet owners, but by veterinary surgeons keen to heal their patients by using more natural forms of medicine and at a more personal level. Homoeopathy and acupuncture have proved popular, with rapidly growing interest in herbal medicine, flower remedies and aromatherapy. Nutrition too has been added to the list, as we realised just how important feeding is to general health. That is not only exactly how and what you feed but also the importance of vitamins, minerals and trace elements. The lesson we have learnt from this is that feeding is as great a part of healing as homoeopathy, herbal medicine and acupuncture is, and that supplements (such as vitamins, minerals and essential fatty acids) have a vital part to play in supporting other natural therapies.

If you have a little time to spare, take a few moments to delve into this book. There is almost certainly something of interest which will help improve the life and health of your cat. Remember that not all cat food has to come out of a tin or packet, so do try some of the recipes to avoid always feeding processed food. Check the lists of natural remedies too; homoeopathic remedies, herbal medicines and flower remedies are safe natural ways of dealing with many of the day to day common feline health problems.

Tim Couzens, MRCVS
Chiddingly, East Sussex

INTRODUCTION

Having written *Canine Care & Cuisine* with Alexandra Bastedo, it was a natural progression to apply the same formula to cats.

I started my research on this book at the pet food section in a local supermarket. Have you ever witnessed people choosing pet food? Dog owners go directly to the brand they always buy, while cat owners diligently study all the labels, before various members of the family are consulted and voice their conflicting views on the culinary likes and dislikes of their feline friend. Observing this confirmed what I had already been told – 'cats are fussy eaters'. No wonder the labels on cat food frequently trumpet 'Improved Recipe' and include phrases like 'With Succulent Pieces of Chicken and Turkey in a Light Gravy' or 'Original Chunks in Nourishing Jelly – Duck and Rabbit Flavour'. It's enough to make one's own mouth water. One feels the pet food manufacturers assume cats can read the labels too – maybe they can, who knows? Anything is possible with a cat. What I was soon to discover was that when it comes to cats, only the best is good enough.

The food combinations intrigued me and fuelled me with ideas. The exciting thing was that when I started inventing and cooking recipes for cats, I was able to make up meals along these lines but without having to use preservatives, sugars and colourants. I could also add more than the standard minimum four per cent of the main ingredient found in most commercial pet foods. I could create tasty dishes at a cheaper price than buying canned or dried cat food. Cooking for your pets as a special treat doesn't have to be a chore; it can be both fun and economical.

Pollyanna
Pickering

Cats and their culinary idiosyncrasies are often mentioned in literature. In selecting the literary quotes for this book, I have been able to give you a small taste of this link ...

Jeannie Kemnitzer
West Sussex, England

FOREWORD

As I start this book there are five tiny kittens in my bathroom, an elderly British Short-Haired Tip and a single orphaned kitten in my study and another eleven cats and nine kittens dotted around the rest of the house and in my specially designed cattery.

I started living with cats eighteen years ago when I married, went to live in a seventeenth-century farmhouse in the country and had an invasion of mice and rats! I couldn't have had a better introduction to the cat world than the nine-month-old black half-Burmese we obtained from Birdham Cat and Guinea Pig Rescue and I have been fascinated by cats ever since.

Kim, as we called him, would indulge in long conversations with me, climb up on to my shoulders where he would groom my hair and purr endlessly with supreme contentment. He also dispensed with the rodents overnight and, as he was somewhat diminutive in size, would chase the rats towards Sophie, our Dobermann, who in turn would toss them into the air and break their necks. It proved a most successful partnership.

We used to take Kim with us on six-mile walks through the fields with our two Dobermanns and retriever, as a result of which he developed rather an adventurous nature. After about a year Kim suddenly disappeared and despite putting 'Missing' notices in shops and newspapers and broadcasting appeals on the radio he was not to be found. We were distraught and for months would wander through the meadows calling his name. I think the dogs understood too, as they sniffed around the bushes trying to get his scent. Kim had slept with them, eaten with them and played with them and in their eyes he had ceased to be a cat and had become an honorary dog. The other result of Kim's absence was that the mice took note and promptly moved back in. Back I went to Cat and Guinea Pig Rescue to see Min Flower, its redoubtable founder, who told me that a cat was less likely to wander if there were two of them, because they would always check up on each other. This time we ended up with Whitey, a middle-aged white stray, and Blackie, a young kitten that had been found on a street in Chichester. We had been advised to get them both on the same day so each would think the other lived there. It worked a treat, as there were no territorial disputes and the two felines became devoted to each other, with Whitey acting as his younger pal's protector against all visiting cats and dogs.

Through my cats I soon became firm friends with Min, and every time I visited her I inevitably fell in love with some new feline that had just arrived. I was particularly taken with strange-looking corduroy-coated creatures which proved to be Cornish Rexes. In no time at all I had a black Cornish Rex of my own called Rexy, a half Rex half Abyssinian called Abbie, a black and white moggie called Coley and the great feline love of my life Hodge, the exquisite talking Tonkinese.

Hodge was a very superior cat, grey with piercing blue eyes, he moved like a panther and spoke like a human: 'Naw' he would say whenever he didn't want something. He soon ended up ruling over the other cats, dogs and us, and a great deal of time was spent catering to his every whim and demand. At night he would creep under my bed covers, and curl up in the crook of my arm purring gently, and as I turned over in my sleep he would roll with me. I had no need for sleeping pills as the contented sound of Hodge beside me always ensured that I had a wonderful night's sleep.

If you love your cats you are familiar with their every hair and their every movement, so when Hodge's skin began to have mini-seizures and his tail started to have an unfamiliar twitch I became concerned. After obtaining different veterinary opinions it finally became clear that Hodge had Feline Aids. 'The prognosis is not good – he has maybe one or two years at the most', the vets said. For some time I had been interested in homoeopathy, herbs and nutrition. I was on an allergy free diet myself taking vitamins, minerals and oil supplements and knew George MacLeod, the pioneer of veterinary homoeopathy at Haywards Heath, through Sophie, my Dobermann, whom he had successfully treated for leaking after a spaying operation. My own alternative medicine doctor came to tea one day and I took the opportunity of asking her about Hodge. 'Yes,' she said, 'you have nothing to lose. With a pure diet and vitamin, mineral and oil supplements you will be able to keep up his immune system and stave off the disease.' I took her advice and gave Hodge good food, nutritional supplements and George MacLeod's homoeopathic remedies every day of his life, and he lived from the age of six to sixteen. I was devastated by his death but consoled by the fact that my vet called him 'geriatric' and said it was unheard of for cats to live that long with the FIV virus.

After Hodge I had a call from Sidlesham Cat Rescue about Sheba the Siamese who was suffering from chronic diarrhoea. She had lived in a flat with lots of dogs and cats and was highly stressed. However, after six weeks in a peaceful environment, eating pure foods and some Hills dry biscuit, she was cured and stayed on to become a permanent member of our household. Another call from Cat Rescue was about Clementine, the tortoiseshell Cornish Rex, who had hardly any hair and also had chronic stomach problems. We treated her with chicken, rabbit, rice and a combination of vitamins, minerals, anti-oxidants and stomach enzymes. It was such a thrill to watch shiny, healthy hair appearing, and considering the bad treatment she had suffered in her past it was amazing that she had such a delightful, chirpy personality. A friend, Wendy Gaye, who already had three Cornish Rexes fell in love with her and, extremely reluctantly, I let her go.

This proved to be the correct decision as she is very happy and now has an extremely glossy coat.

Duchess the white moggie (who was only nine months old herself) and her four tiny kittens were next to be taken in and they were all very sick indeed. There is a limit to how much antibiotic can be pumped into a kitten so the answer was alternative medicines. I started with diced chicken and rice, with children's liquid vitamins and stomach enzymes, and progressed to colloidal minerals, vitamins and anti-oxidants. A little liver from time to time was very beneficial, and organic porridge and a small amount of live goats' yoghurt with wheatgerm also went down well. After them I took in many more sick orphaned kittens and found it was particularly important to keep them warm and clean as they had no mother to look after them. The last cats who came to us at the end of the kitten season were Negra and her four black and white kittens. They were all sick after eating and it seemed likely that the problem was worms as they filled out quickly after deworming, and the vomiting also stopped.

At no point did I feed my cats canned food as the colourants, additives and preservatives in some tins might have made them sicker. I cooked all the time: fish, rabbit, chicken, turkey and occasional liver with a few cooked vegetables and predominantly either brown rice or millet. It was hard work but extremely rewarding, and by the time they went on to their new homes they were all extremely fit, glossy-coated cats.

The culmination of all this nutritional work, under the guidance of my homoeopathic vet Mark Elliott, was a conversation with him in which I bemoaned the lack of special quality vitamins for my dogs and cats. As a result Mark Elliott formulated the Feline Care range for my company Pet Nutrition Concepts Ltd. I had always wanted to be a vet myself, but at least now with healthy cooked food and special cat vitamins, minerals, anti-oxidants and essential oils I can avoid large vets' bills, and I can give all my rescued cats the nutritional foods and supplements that they both need and deserve.

Alexandra Bastedo
West Sussex, England

xiv

ACKNOWLEDGEMENTS

Grateful thanks to:

Mark Elliott, our homoeopathic vet and Nick Thompson, Meg Kaplan and Peter Brown, his associates, for all their advice, care and approval and for helping to make my cats long-lived, healthy senior citizens.

Francis Hunter VetMFHom, MRCVS, chairman of the British Homoeopathic Association for sharing his extensive knowledge with us.

Tim Couzens BVet Med, MRCVS, VetMFHom for all his useful tips.

The Reverend David MacLeod for his kindness and help.

Min Flower, the doyenne of pet rescue who introduced me to my first cat, Kim, and who taught me about cat rescue.

Monique Turk and Nigel Oddy of Sidlesham Cat and Rabbit Rescue and Feralands for all their help and advice over the years and for completing my cat rescue education, with all its ups and downs, warts and all.

Jennie Parkhouse of Shirrin Persian Cat Rescue for all her advice on pedigree long-hairs and Persians.

Susan Luxford-Watts for teaching me all I know about Cornish Rexes.

Sandy Charlwood for her care, tenderness and help with our rescued, sickly kittens.

Jessie Howling and Bob Hutchins without whose special constant help our animal rescue operation would not be possible, also our volunteers Helen, Francesca and Juliette.

Richard Farhall, the managing director of the Vegan Society, for generously allowing us to reprint their recipes in The Vegetarian/ Vegan Victuals chapter.

HOLISTIC HEALING

'Our food should be our medicine and our medicine should be our food'

Hippocrates

1

Feline holistic healing is the treatment of cats with natural remedies: homoeopathy, herbs and nutrition. A qualified vet should be consulted whenever necessary, and surgery carried out or the appropriate drug prescribed, but in my opinion antibiotics and steroids are used far too often when a natural remedy may suffice. Too much chemical medication can lower the immune system and destroy the natural flora in the gut. If the right foods are given, along with the correct nutrients and preventative homoeopathic and herbal remedies, unless there is a genetic fault or serious injury, I believe that vets' bills can be kept to a minimum.

My veterinary gurus are George MacLeod – who was to the forefront of homoeopathy when I came across him seventeen years ago – Francis Hunter, Tim Couzens, Dr Richard Pitcairn and my own vet Mark Elliott. It is with their help and with reference to their books (listed in the bibliography at the back of the book) that I have compiled the section on homoeopathy. I also swear by Juliette de Bairacli Levy, Tim Couzens and Diane Stein's herbal remedies, which can work very well with felines. Nutritionally cats are very complicated and different from dogs, and for that reason they should never be fed dry commercial dog food, poor quality protein such as offal, or a vegetarian diet without specific supplements. Cats require taurine, glycine, calcium, phosphorus and vitamin E, which wild cats would find in their prey and which they would eat raw. Any cooking should not be overdone as the above vital ingredients will be destroyed if heat levels are high. Francis Hunter says carbohydrates should never make up more than 30–40 per cent of the diet, fat 20 per cent and protein 35–40 per cent with taurine 0.28 per cent–0.32 per cent. According to the American vet Dr Pitcairn, the daily taurine content of wild cat's prey is 25-50 milligrams, so there is no problem if meat is fed raw, but if it is cooked up to 80 per cent of the taurine can be lost, dropping to 12–35 milligrams per meal per day, so it may be advisable to supplement. Taurine capsules can be found in most good health food shops. A ten-pound cat can eat as much as 60–80 milligrams of taurine in its food each day. Dr Pitcairn and Mark Elliott both recommend adding feline vitamins and minerals to the cat's diet, and these should be added at the end of the cooking process.

Samuel Hahnemann, the founder of homoeopathy, said that

homoeopathy was curative rather than preventative and that one had to abide by the laws of nature. Homoeopathy could not cure if the underlying cause was bad nutrition.

KEY HOMOEPATHIC REMEDIES

These are just a few of the homoeopathic remedies available for our cats. For more detailed information as to the appropriate remedy and dosage please consult a homoeopathic vet (they are listed at the end of the book). Alternatively invest in George MacLeod's, Francis Hunter's, Tim Couzens', Dr Richard Pitcairn's or Mark Elliott's homoeopathic books.

If you are a sceptic or question the value of homoeopathy, the time to turn to it is when conventional medicine has failed and you have nothing to lose. I have often been amazed at the successes I have had using homoeopathy on my numerous cats. It is definitely *not* mumbo jumbo and given the correct remedy it can work miracles when all other avenues have failed.

Cats are notoriously difficult to administer remedies to and I have been scratched and bitten on many an occasion. The obvious thing is to try and hide the remedy in food, but if you don't succeed I suggest you use a pill popper, a syringe (if liquid) or crush the pill to a powder, put it in the fold of a small piece of paper and tip it down the throat. A finger can be used but you have to be brave and quick in pushing a tablet or capsule down a cat's gullet. Homoeopathic remedies are available from more enlightened pharmacies, health food shops and some pet stores. If you are fit you will find that kneeling and jamming the cat between your knees is the best position in which to administer pills, as it leaves both your hands free. It may also help to wrap the cat in a towel like a strait-jacket, thereby immobilising its sharp claws.

There may be occasions when a homoeopathic remedy does not work, in which case your holistic vet may well advise a conventional medicine or surgery. The important thing is that you get your cat well by whatever means possible, whether homoeopathic, herbal or conventional.

CONDITION	REMEDY
ABSCESSES	*Streptococcus* is the principal remedy *Hepar Sulph* is for painful infection and suppuration. According to Francis Hunter it could be considered the homoeopathic equivalent of an anti-biotic, as its action is principally directed at infected tissues and glands. *Silicea* should be considered if a pain-less splinter or foreign body may be involved
ALOPECIA (Hair loss)	*Thallium Acetas, Nat Mur* and *Thyroidium* are the major remedies.
ANAEMIA	According to George MacLeod this is difficult to treat homoeopathically. He suggests: *Arsenicum Album* which may help damage done to red blood cells. *Crotalus Horr* and *Lachesis* where there are liver problems or jaundice. *Cinchona* can supplement other remedies where there is weakness and lethargy due to loss of body fluid. *Ferrum Metallicum*, or *Ferrum Iodum* or *Ferum Muriaticum* should be given in case of an iron deficiency.
ANAEMIA (Can be caused by heavy infestations of fleas.)	*Aconitum, Arnica, Ficus Religiosa* and *Ipecac* are just some of the remedies suggested by George MacLeod.
ARTHRITIS	*Rhus Tox* is particularly good where restlessness is a problem. *Bryonia* is often beneficial in chronic arthritis and can be followed by *Rhus Tox*, or the remedies may be alternated once or twice daily.
BRONCHITIS	*Bryonia* is good for chest infections and many kinds of cough. Other remedies which may be appropriate are:

CONDITION	REMEDY
	Antimonium Tart for frothy mucus.
	Apis Mel when there is fluid mucus. *Coccus Cacti* with spasmodic coughing. *Kali Bich* for yellow mucus. *Rumax* or *Spongia* for older animals with heart problems. *Scilla* with vomiting
CONJUNCTIVITIS	*Arg Nit, Pulsatilla, Euphrasia, Hypericum* and *Calendula* (diluted 1/40) can be given in water as an eye bath.
CONSTIPATION	Mark Elliott recommends: *Aesculus Hippocastanum* to assist the cat which is suffering a large, hard, dry stool with sharp fragments, such as bones or eaten cat litter, which is painful to pass; *Alumina* is also good. *Antimonium Crud* for constipation alternating with diarrhoea. *Nux Vom* for frequent ineffectual urging, often following a dietary indiscretion. *Opium* for constipation with absence of desire for stool. If passed the stool is of round, hard, black balls. *Silica* when the stool is dry and passed with great difficulty, which often, when partially expelled, slips back in.
	George MacLeod recommends: *Alumen* is applicable when there is also sickness. *Bryonia* is appropriate when there are hard dark stools. *Lycopodium* should be given when there are liver or breathing difficulties as well. *Nat Mur* is for general debilitation. *Nux Vom* is for digestive problems generally.
CYSTITIS	There are several possibilities: *Cantharis, Urtica Urens, Uva Ursi, Sasparilla* and *Causticum* in difficult cases. *Merc Cor* may be appropriate for severe cases.

CONDITION	REMEDY
DIABETES	According to Francis Hunter *Syzygium Jumbul* can be a very effective remedy, as is *uranium*.
DIARRHOEA, DIGESTIVE PROBLEMS AND ENTERITIS	In severe cases or with haemorrhaging *China Officinalis* and *Croton Tiglium* should be given. *Morgan Gaertner* cured Cardy, my white Cornish Rex, who had suffered from a vomiting disorder for a long time. *Nux Vomica* has also been successful with my sick cats. *Podophyllum* is also effective. *Phosphorus* should normally be given if there is vomiting and pain. *Camphora* may be useful for enteritis caused by salmonella. *Aloes* may help spluttery jelly-like diarrhoea.
EARS	*Malandrium* may help some forms of ear mites. Also *Calendula* diluted 1/20 in water. *Aconitum* and *Hepar Sulph* are appropriate for inflammation of the middle ear. *Pulsatilla* is also very effective.
EPILEPSY	*Belladonna, Arnica, Cocculus, Nat Sulph, Opium* and *Tarentula Hispanica* are the main remedies. *Silica* may also be used.
EYE CONDITIONS	*Cineraria Maritima* can be given diluted 1/10 in water. *Hippozaenium* may help the tear-filled eyes due to cat flu.
EYE INJURIES	Give *Ledum Palustre*.
FLEAS	*Sulphur* may make the animal less attractive to fleas.
GUMS AND TEETH	*Calc Fluor* may be helpful for abscesses. *Fragaria* helps in dissolving tartar. *Merc Viv* is useful for gingivitis.
HEART	If there is a respiratory problem *Spongia Tosta* can be of use. *Cactus* and *crataegus* are good supportive remedies.

7

CONDITION	REMEDY
HAEMORRHAGING	If slow give *Crotalus Horr* and if fast give *Ipecacuanha*. *Arnica* can also be of use.
INFERTILITY	*Sepia* is particularly helpful to females and *Pulsatilla* is good for the ovaries. *Platina* is often the most appropriate for the Siamese breed.
INJURIES	For general injuries give *Arnica* or *Symphytum*. *Hypericum* may help pain. *Bellis* is good if the pelvis is involved.
LARYNGITIS	Give *Aconitum*, *Apis Mel*, *Rhus Tox*, or *Baryta Carb*. *Silicea* can be administered in extreme cases. *Ferrum Phos* is an important remedy.
LUNGS	For fluid on the lung give *Apis Mel*, *Crataegus* or *Adonis Vert*.
MATERNAL INSTINCT	*Sepia Officinalis* may help with queens that are not interested in their kittens. *Staphisagria* will help those that ignore them after a difficult birth, as will *Platina*.
MISCARRIAGES	*Viburnum Opulis* or *Plumbum* should help in establishing a normal pregnancy. In the young *Calc Phos* is particularly good.
OSTEOPOROSIS	*Calcarea Fluor* hardens bone. *Hecla Lava* and *Silicea* can also help.
PANCREATIC PROBLEMS	*Iris Vers*, *Iodum*, or *Gaertner* are some of the remedies that may be administered.
PLEURISY	*Aconitum*, *Belladonna*, *Bryonia* or *Arsen Alb* are the appropriate remedies.
PNEUMONIA	*Aconitum*, *Bryonia*, *Arsen Iod*, *Ipecac*, *Kali Carb* or *Phosphorus* could be given.
PREGNANCY	*Viburnum Opulis* is good for the first few weeks. *Arnica* or *Ipecac* may help prevent haemorrhaging.

CONDITION	REMEDY
RESPIRATORY PROBLEMS	*Rumex Crispus* is useful in many instances.
RHINITIS	*Arsenicum Album, Pulsatilla* or *Kali Bich* are the main remedies.
SHOCK	*Aconite* and *Arnica* are the best remedies. Bach Rescue Remedy, one or two drops on the tongue, is also excellent for shock, stress and travel nerves. It can also revive weak kittens at birth.
SICKNESS	For sea sickness give *Tabacum Tobacco*. For car sickness give *Cocculus* or *Petroleum*.
SINUSITIS (With nasal discharge)	*Hepar Sulph, Silicea* or *Lemna Minor* may help.
SKIN CONDITIONS	Give *Sulphur*. This is particularly good for mange, eczema and other skin problems.
SPLEEN PROBLEMS	*Ceonothus* is the appropriate remedy.
SPRAYING	If territorial *Ustillago Maydis* should be given to a male cat. If spraying occurs after neutering *Staphisagria* can be given to males or females. Extra hormone doses such as *Folliculinum, Ovarium, Oestrogen* and *Testosterone* may also be beneficial.
STROKES	*Aconitum, Bufo, Arnica* or *Conium* are useful remedies.
THROMBOSIS	*Crotalus, Lachesis*, or *Vipera* should be given.
TONSILLITIS	*Aconitum, Belladonna* or *Rhus Tox* may be beneficial. In chronic cases *Baryta Carb* and *Hepar Sulph* can be administered.
WARTS	*Thuja Occidentalis* should help; nitric acid if they bleed.

CONDITION	REMEDY
WOUNDS	Open wounds can benefit from *Hypericum Perforatum* along with *Calendula Officinalis*. *Calendula* is also excellent when used as a cream after spaying. I also employed it safely on an orphaned tabby kitten with a sore bottom. Puncture wounds, insect bites and eye injuries should be treated with *Ledum Palustre*. Septic wounds may benefit from *Chininum Sulphuricum*. Echinacea is also good for septic conditions. Lachesis is also effective.

TRUSTED TIPS

1. Do get your new kitten or cat inoculated whether conventionally or homoeopathically before you allow it to go outside and mix with other cats, particularly if you live in a built-up area.

2. Vaccinations are an object of dispute. They can harm and they can kill. Make sure your animal is in optimum condition before vaccinating. I had to wait a long time before I deemed young Alfie, my long-haired rescue cat, to be well enough for his first vaccination. He was finally done at seven months. The normal ages for vaccinations are nine weeks and twelve weeks but I prefer fourteen and seventeen if possible. Also be aware of over-vaccinating (*see* Healthy Hints A–Z).

3. Do provide enough toys for your kitten's 'mad moments'. Crisp boxes or cardboard boxes with holes make excellent playhouses, ping pong balls, emery boards, feathers bound together with an elastic band and small objects tied to bits of string can give endless hours of pleasure.

4. On no account give aspirin or any similar medication. Dogs' metabolisms are much more like humans' but cats' are very different. Do not presume that medication for you will suit the cat, quite the contrary – it may kill.

5. Do not overfeed. Overfeeding can cause diarrhoea in kittens and obese cats are unfit cats. Any food that is left should always be removed and either thrown away or put in the refrigerator and kept for one more serving.

6. Do not use Dettol or, in general, any disinfectant that changes colour when in contact with water as you may seriously damage your cat. Also avoid carpet fresheners, which may be toxic to cats.

7. If your cat tumbles into oil you can remove it with a bath of mild washing-up liquid – it worked a treat when Blackie my moggie fell into oil, but be careful to avoid the eyes.

8. Cats should be shampooed with gentle baby shampoos. Corpore Sano anti-parasite shampoo and tonic works well on

Sheba, my Siamese, who is allergic to almost every flea product. However, unless the cat lives in a grimy inner-city or is particularly prone to fleas, it should not be necessary to shampoo often, if at all.

9. Don't keep plants like azaleas, chrysanthemums, cyclamens, holly leaves, mistletoe, oleander or poinsettias as they can be poisonous to felines.

10. Try and give liver once or twice a week as it contains folic acid, but not too much as it can cause diarrhoea.

11. Garlic or brewers' yeast added to food can help keep away fleas. However brewers' yeast should not be given to cats with a less than robust digestive system.

12. A garlic clove should not be given at the same time of day as vitamins and minerals. It is very strong and can diminish their efficacity.

13. *Silica* is the homoeopathic remedy for removing splinters or thorns.

14. For inflamed eyes bathe with raw cucumber juice, or *euphrasia* diluted 1 to 20 parts water.

15. Honey and ginger are good for travel sickness. The homoeopathic remedies are *Tabacum, Petroleum* or *Cocculus Indicus*; *Pulsatilla* and *Bach Scleranthus* also help.

16. One or two drops of Bachs Rescue Remedy is excellent for countering stress in a cat, it is also excellent for journeys. For an extremely nervous cat it often helps to partially cover the cat carrier with a blanket.

17. Do beware of canned foods containing un-named preservatives, additives, colourants and caramels. Sugar rots the teeth and most of the middle-aged cats I have rescued have had to have tooth extractions. I also find that as a cat gets older its digestive system gets less robust and it needs purer, unadulterated food with vitamin and mineral supplements, oils, anti-oxidants and, sometimes, stomach enzymes as well.

13

18. Semi-moist foods contain the most preservatives and the most sugars; personally I prefer cans or dried biscuit for my cats.

19. Are cats really meant to eat nothing but cereal nuggets? I think all-in-one biscuits are very good as tooth cleaners but I have my reservations about feeding them as a sole food, based on personal experience. If a cat eats dried food it needs to drink water in order not to dehydrate and ruin the kidneys. Some cats don't like drinking – which is why I lost my lovely black and white moggie, Coley, from kidney failure. As with cans it is an unfortunate fact of life that the more expensive products are normally better than the cheap ones.

20. If you are feeding low quality foods your cat's immune system may be helped with feline vitamins and minerals, anti-oxidants and essential oils.

21. Ground eggshell sprinkled on to your cat's food is a good source of calcium (calcium carbonate) which will aid bone building.

22. If you want to stop a cat fight do not go into the mêlée with bare hands; the cats will simply think you are a third cat come to join the battle and turn on you. (One friend who did so ended up in Casualty having a tetanus jab and several stitches!) The best way to separate two warring fiends is either with a spray or a bucket of water. If neither is available a rug thrown over the assailant will immobilise the offender and sometimes a commanding loud vocal sound is sufficient. When Hodge my Tonkinese and Coley my black and white moggie came to blows in the utility room, Jessie, my assistant, was able to pin one down with a mop while throwing a bucket of water over the other – it worked a treat. After that they still came to blows occasionally but never when in the vicinity of a mop and bucket!

23. If your cat has a serious disease like Feline Infectious Peritonitis (FIP), Feline Leukaemia (FeLV), Feline Aids (FIV) or cancer and the prognosis is said to be poor do *not* give up.

Pure cooked foods, occasional liver and large doses of feline vitamins, minerals, anti-oxidants, essential oils and stomach enzymes can help.

24. If your cat looks like getting cat flu make sure it is kept warm, but that the room is well aired and not too hot. Two of my cats, Blackie and Whitey, went down with cat flu when they insisted on being with my eighty-four-year-old father-in-law, who liked his room to be at 80°C. They only recovered when they were banned from his room.

25. Do not be surprised at your own grief over the death of your cat. It will have been a family member and part of your life, hopefully, for several years. I find I need to talk to other caring cat owners who understand the need to grieve and appreciate notes of condolence. I too send cards of sympathy when friends' animals die. There is no doubt the loss of a pet hurts, and the lack of their presence cannot lightly be dismissed. The homoeopathic remedy *Ignatia* can be given to both humans and animals who are grieving. Rescue Remedy can be used short-term.

26. Do make a will as many cats end up in rescue centres when their owners die. If you make some financial provision for your cat after you have gone, it should ensure that your cat is well looked after.

IF YOU HAVE...

- If you have a state-of-the-art computer think twice before leaving it alone with your cat. A little feline walk along the computer keyboards and you may find all the programmes have been zapped!

- If you have a member of the family who has an allergy to cats, have you ever thought of getting a Cornish Rex? They are known as the 'poodle cat' and have fur like corduroy which may be more easily tolerated. They have delightful, affectionate dispositions and are very athletic cats. However, you may want to check if their allergies are food-related. I used to have chronic hay fever and was allergic to my Abyssinian cross, Abbie, until I gave up dairy products and ate only organic, old-fashioned wheat. I no longer have a problem. Other less allergy-causing cats are the Devon Rex and the hairless Sphinx.

- If you have a new baby be careful about giving your cat unsupervised access to the baby in its cot or pram. In the winter months a baby will have the appeal of a mini-electric blanket. Children under the age of three should not, as a general rule, be left unsupervised with animals.

- If you have to move house be careful not to upset your cat, as this is a time when many cats escape the commotion of the removal man and disappear. The best thing is to keep them locked in a room (possibly the bathroom where there is no furniture) until you are ready to transfer them to your cat carrier and their new abode. The cats should then be kept locked in the new house for a fortnight. If a cat is particularly terrified it is sensible to confine it to one room initially. However beware of the unexpected: a friend lost his white moggie up the chimney on the first day of the move. Three days later a black cat descended! The Bach Flower Remedy walnut can help a cat to cope with changes in its life.

- If you have moved within a six-mile radius of your old home you may have a problem. In Cat Rescue we never re-home within that radius, as the cat always returns to its original territory. To counter that dilemma you may have to keep the cat in for much longer than two weeks.

- If you live in a high rise flat it is advisable to instal summer screens in the windows as there have been many instances of cats falling from high buildings.

- If you have a cat that has smelly faeces try putting it on a pure diet. Suki, the half-Burmese I rescued, went on strike and would only eat pure chicken (with vitamin and mineral powders) and as a result she only used her cat litter every other day. When I consulted the vet he said that what she was eating was so pure that most of it was being used up by the body and very little was coming out the other end! And what there was hardly smelt at all!

- If you have a cat whose hair stands up on its back it may be a sign of illness so you should seek veterinary attention.

- If you have a cat that suddenly starts to drink a lot it may have a kidney problem so it should be taken to your vet post-haste.

- If you have an indoor cat do grow some coltsfoot grass in a pot in the house and give barley grass, Greensmore or Feline Care Vitamins and Minerals. An outdoor cat will have access to and eat grasses and vegetation, so you should try and provide some form of greens for your indoor cat.

- If you have a sick kitten, ask your vet for a stool test as soon as possible as the kitten may have parasites, which can kill.

A TO Z OF
HEALTHY HINTS

The following tips for various health-related problems are based on nutrition and herbs. For easy reference, I have included some of the homoeopathic remedies again here.

A is For:

ABSCESSES

To have less chance of suffering from abscesses caused by fights the animals should be neutered.

Homoeopathically: *Lachesis Muta* should be given immediately as a single dose for preventative measures and *Silicea* should be given when the abscess is fully formed. *Streptococcus* and *Hepar Sulph* are also important remedies.

Herbally: Echinacea helps to purify and boost the immune system and I have had success with putting honey and chlorella powder poultices on the abscesses.

ACUPUNCTURE

Acupuncture can have remarkable results with slipped discs, arthritis, epilepsy and many other problems. A cat was recently taken to see my vet, hissing and yowling with pain. The vet located the problem in the spine (the cat had one leg shorter than the others after an accident) and when he lasered the acupuncture points the animal became very calm and fell asleep on the surgery table. Peter Brown the Australian vet and acupuncturist treated a ginger cat that had radial nerve paralysis in one leg after being impaled on a fence. The cat couldn't move the leg at all, but after three acupuncture sessions was totally cured.

AIDS, FELINE (FIV)

At first the diagnosis can be depressing as the general prognosis is poor. However, if caught in time you can boost the cat's immune system to such an extent that the disease virtually disappears. Hodge, my Tonkinese, started to have mini-seizures at the onset of this condition and after talking to my alternative medicine doctor

I decided to bombard him with all the vitamins and minerals given to human AIDS patients. Although similar, humans CANNOT catch Aids from cats. I gave him 1000 mg vitamin C, kelp, zinc, vitamin E, fish oils, calcium, vitamin B complex, organic garlic and a feline multi vitamin mineral complex twice weekly. He was only given the purest, organic foods and had cooked chicken liver twice weekly. With a disease like Feline Aids you have nothing to lose and Hodge, as I mentioned earlier, lived from the age of six, when it was diagnosed, to the age of sixteen, which I gather is something of a record.

Homoeopathically: *Marble, Magnesium, Phosphorus, Silica* and the FIV nosode may help.

Herbally: Echinacea and Coenzyme Q10 (10 mg) can also help boost the immune system, as can Burdock.

ANAEMIA

Anaemia can be caused by incorrect nutrition, or an infestation of fleas sucking the cat's blood. Recently I came across a case of a kitten that had so little blood left by the fleas that a vet actually had to give it a blood transfusion. It may also be a sign of leukaemia. In the case of worms or fleas the appropriate remedy should be used.

If the anaemia is due to wrong feeding a little lamb or chicken liver should be given twice a week, as well as broccoli, oats, kelp, vitamin C powder (up to 1000 milligrams per day for a large cat), brewers' yeast (vitamin Bs) and feline multi vitamins and minerals.

Homoeopathically: *China Officinalis* could be given and *Ferrum Metallicum* where there is an iron deficiency.

Herbally: Echinacea is an excellent immune system booster. It should not be used all the time as it works better when given in fortnightly (daily) bursts. Nettles are a good source of iron.

ANTI-OXIDANTS

Feline Care anti-oxidants are designed to be a real weapon in the fight against damage to the body by pollutants, chemicals in food, stress and age deterioration. Anti-oxidants may help in the treatment of allergies, arthritis, cancer, heart disease, cataracts, liver disease, skin problems and viral infections amongst others. The anti-oxidant activity is formed by a combination of vitamins A, C, E, selenium and herbs, including echinacea, for its immune system boosting capabilities.

ANXIETY

First try to work out the cause of the anxiety and try to rectify the situation.

Homoeopathically: *Aconite, Arsen Alb, Gelsemium, Nux Vom* and *Arg Nit* can help calm down a nervous animal. Anxiety when moving house is often alleviated by the homoeopathic remedies *Capsicum* 6c or *Phosphorus Acid* 6c four times daily for seven to ten days.

Herbally: Agrimony, valerian, skullcap and aspen can be beneficial. Tim Couzens and Grace McHatty recommend Bach remedy red chestnut for cats who are nervous when put in a cattery while my vet advocates many of the Bach Flower Remedies, and Bach Rescue Remedy is excellent for fearful travellers. The Bach Flower Remedy honeysuckle may also be helpful and walnut is suggested for stress due to change.

ARTHRITIS

Plump cats should immediately be put on a pure diet to lose weight. Extra calcium or bonemeal should be added to food, and oils such as vitamin E daily and a little cod liver oil twice a week along with vitamin C may be beneficial. (It is important never to overdose cod liver oil so a quarter of a teaspoon is sufficient). Nutritionally vitamin C, A and D and E supplements are the most beneficial and collagen supplements could be useful.

Homoeopathically: *Rhus Tox* is the most commonly used remedy and *Bryonia* and *Pulsatilla* may also help. For older cats try *Arnica*.

Herbally: Nettles can be very effective; Alfalfa and garlic may help.

B is For:

BAD BREATH

In the cases of Byron and Camilla (who were ten and eight respectively when I took them on) both had bad breath and both had bad teeth which had to be extracted by the vet. The condition may have been caused by the sugar in some commercial foods. In the case of Cardy, my white Cornish Rex, the halitosis was caused by an ongoing stomach problem. This was cured by the homoeopathic remedy *Morgan Gaertner* and also by adding stomach-enzyme powder (kept in the refrigerator) to his food. Liquid vitamins and minerals are more absorbable for an upset stomach. Cat biscuits can make good tooth cleaners or – use a toothbrush!

Homoeopathically: *Calc Fluor* is good for tooth and gum disorders. *Morgan Gaertner* can help when halitosis is due to stomach problems. *Nux Vomica* or *Rhus Tox* can be useful.

Herbally: Garlic and alfalfa in food may work.

BELLIGERENCE

Homoeopathically: *Hyoscyamus* and *Staphisagria* are two of the best remedies for aggressive, territorial cats.

Herbally: The most calming herbs are valerian and skullcap; Larch is also very effective. Bachs Rescue Remedy can be given to the victim of the intimidation.

BURNS

Internally give vitamin B (in complex form) C, E, fish oils (A and D) and zinc. Also internally Bachs Rescue Remedy or a couple of drops of brandy in half a teaspoon of liquid honey can be helpful if the cat is in shock.

Homoeopathically: Externally *Urtica Urens* diluted in water can be put on a bandage and kept damp on the affected area or calendula can be smoothed on. The homoeopathic remedy *Cantharis* can be given internally.

C is For:

CANCER

Early diagnosis is most important so do keep an eye out for subtle changes in your cat. When Snowdrop (a feral who had been living behind dustbins) arrived she had nasty black ears which proved to be cancerous. Ginger and white cats are particularly vulnerable to ear cancer and should either be kept inside when the sun is at its strongest or have sunblock put on their ears. When I managed to feel Snowdrop's tummy I also detected lumps on her nipples. These also proved to be cancerous and they were surgically removed. The prognosis was not good. I then bombarded her with large doses of vitamin C, vitamin E, fish oils, zinc, selenium, feline multi vitamins and minerals and anti-oxidant, organic garlic and echinacea and she is still here four years later. The above vitamin, mineral and herbal remedies are good immune system boosters for all forms of cancer. Juliette de Bairacli Levy recommends turnip, aloe vera and grape juice as well. On no account should the animal be given commercial cat foods, as some are full of colourants, additives, sugars, preservatives and chemicals. The other extremely important factor for the animal is no stress, so see if you can give your pet a calm but not too sedentary life as exercise can also be beneficial.

COLDS

At the onset of sneezing my cats are the recipients of vitamin C (powder or capsules) and zinc, as well as Feline Care multi vitamin-multi minerals and anti-oxidants to boost the immune system. Sometimes I put echinacea drops diluted with water in a syringe, and administer that too. When Cardy, the white Cornish Rex, was very nasally congested I also put some Olbas oil on the edge of one of his beds and a little eucalyptus oil on the edge of the other. Tiger balm at a safe distance can also help clear the nasal passages. However none of these oils should be put right next to the nose. You can also put your cat in the bathroom when you are having a hot bath as the steam can help congestion.

Homoeopathically: Meg Kaplan has given my cats a homoeopathic sinusitis mix consisting of: *Pulsatilla 3x, Hydrastis 3x* and

Kali Bich 6x. This remedy has worked well on Coco my brown and white Cornish Rex, who seemed to have a permanent cold until Meg's concoction cured him.

CONSTIPATION

Constipation can be due to nerves or wrong feeding. Cook pure foods and add oat bran, organic garlic and a little extra virgin olive oil. Powdered stomach enzymes can also be helpful in correcting the balance of different floras in the gut. Raw rabbit and a touch of raw grated broccoli would be a good diet to get things moving. Vitamins E, C and zinc should also be given.

Homoeopathically: *Aesculus Hippocastanum, Nux Vom, Opium, Plumbum* and *Silica* are just some of the remedies that may be helpful. (*See* the homoeopathic section for other possibilities.)

COUGHS

Vitamin C is most important, so at the first cough or sneeze I always give my cats between 500 and 1000 mg a day, depending on the size of the cat. Vitamins A and D or fish oil should be given twice weekly (always be careful not to overdose A and D). Vitamin E works at its optimum level when combined with fish oil, and selenium and zinc are also excellent immune system boosters.

Herbally: The best herbs for coughing are liquorice, marshmallow, garlic, echinacea and peppermint.

D is For:

DIABETES

The first thing to look at with diabetes is what you are feeding your animal and whether it contains sugars (often called caramels) and preservatives. If you don't know you can always call the pet food manufacturer (*see* Appropriate Addresses) and ask them. However, to be absolutely sure there is no sugar in the food, it is obviously better to indulge in home-cooking. The cat should have two light meals a day, always at the same time to keep up the blood sugar levels. Protein should be from lean meat, some fish, vegetables (particularly green beans) and millet, rice, oats and polenta. All the B vitamins and C are very important and vitamin E may help with deteriorating eyesight. The minerals zinc and chromium may also be useful.

Homoeopathically: Dr Richard Pitcairn recommends *Natrum Muriaticum 6x* and Francis Hunter particularly advocates *Syzigium Jambolanum*. The suggested potency of 3x of the latter can be given three times daily and can actually help to reduce the amount of insulin given, and in some mild cases it may replace the insulin altogether.

Herbally: Dandelion, seaweed and organic garlic are beneficial.

DEATH

If death comes naturally *Arsenicum Album* can aid the animal's passage by calming it down. Tim Couzens recommends Aconite when there is extreme agitation and restlessness. He says a few doses of aconite given at timely intervals can make a vast difference. Choosing euthanasia can be very difficult and personally I find judging the right moment agonising, but often necessary. I believe that quality of life is all, and that if you can offer a way out to a pet that is suffering with no hope of recovery, then you should take it. This is not for three-legged cats who often live minus one limb very happily for years, but for fatally ill cats that are in distress. However, I do believe in asking for a pre-med shot so that the animal is already asleep and not upset by the lethal injection. If you choose to let the cat die naturally you should not force feed it, just give water and keep it quiet and warm, perhaps with its litter tray nearby. Dr Richard Pitcairn, the American vet, also recommends *Arsenicum Album 30c* for 90 per cent of dying animals. He suggests *Pulsatilla 30c* for an animal that is complaining and calling out or wanting to be held. A vet should be called to animals who are in agony, extremely agitated and screaming out in pain; but if he or she is a long time coming *Tarentula Cubensis 30c* is a useful remedy to give. If you are taking your animal to the vet Bachs Rescue Remedy can also calm the animal down.

DIARRHOEA

This can be caused by a worm infestation, allergies, rotten food, bacteria and viruses. The most important thing is to fast the animal for twenty-four hours but make sure it is drinking water to avoid dehydration. After that you can give a little live goats' yoghurt or stomach enzymes with a little white rice and free range breast of chicken. Beware giving milk, as a lactose intolerance may actually contribute to the problem. Also remove any chemical flea collars and stop using flea products while the condition persists.

Homoeopathically: There are a number of remedies which can help. Apart from those already mentioned in the homoeopathic section, Pitcairn suggests *Podophyllum 6c* for typical diarrhoea and *Mercurius Corrosivus 6c* for dysentery often with straining and bloody stools. *Arsenicum Album 6c* should be given after bad meat and *Natrum Muriaticum 6x* for longer lasting diarrhoea, particularly when the cat sits hunched up on all fours after eating. *Pulsatilla 6c* may be given when cats have binged or eaten food that is too rich for them.

Herbally: Slippery elm powder and roasted carob powder should be given.

I have also given children's (not adults') Kaolin to my sick kittens. However if the condition continues you must consult a holistic vet. It wasn't until Mark Elliott suggested that Alfie, the kitten, had a rare allergy to chicken that we managed to cure his diarrhoea. If you suspect a food allergy you should try removing one kind of food at a time for four days to see if the problem stops.

E is For:

EAR MITES

A solution which works very well is a quarter ounce of extra virgin olive oil mixed with 200 iu of vitamin E. This should be massaged in the ear canal and excess oil should be removed gently with a cotton bud. The treatment should be given on alternate days over a week. A Corpore Sano anti-parasite shampoo may also be a good idea if you suspect the mites are outside the ear as well. Pat McKay in her book *Reigning Cats and Dogs* recommends cleaning the ear with a solution which is 50 per cent witch hazel and 50 per cent water.

Homoeopathically: *Malandrium* may help ear mites and calendula diluted 1/10 in water. *Aconitum* and *Hepar Sulph* are good for inflammation of the middle ear, and *Merc Cor* or *Rhus Tox* should be given in the case of severe ear infection. Very inflamed ears respond to *Belladonna. Pulsatilla* is also good.

Herbally: An infusion of rumex crispus can be given twice a week for a month; *Plantain* and *Echinacea* can be effective.

EPILEPSY

Epilepsy is less common in cats than dogs but can happen nonetheless. The most likely cause is a head injury and some vets now suspect vaccination. Diet is important in epilepsy and only the purest foods, like chicken and rice, should be given, alternated with vegetables or a Vegecat vegan diet. A vitamin B complex which is excellent for nerves and vitamin C and zinc will also help.

Homoeopathically: *Belladonna* and *Stramonium* are probably the first remedies to try, particularly when the animals have dilated pupils and try to escape from their surroundings. George MacLeod recommends *Cocculus 6c* as a remedy which can be used long term and may prevent seizures. He also suggests *Nat Sulph, Opium* and *Tarentula Hispanica. Silica* is also good.

Herbally: Skullcap and valerian are calming remedies for shattered nerves and Bachs Rescue Remedy can also help bring round an animal and calm its fear.

ESSENTIAL ACIDS

Essential fatty acids are increasingly being recognised as an important part of a cat's diet. They are vital for cell membranes and cell function throughout the body. Omega-3 essential fatty acids have beneficial effects on cardiovascular function, arthritis and other inflammatory conditions including eczema, dry skin or poor coat, mental deterioration and nerve problems.

Omega6 can help skin conditions, hair loss, fatigue, anaemia, kidney degeneration, liver problems and arthritis. When spirulina and chlorella are added to the oils they help to boost the immune system and detoxify the liver, blood and bowels from chemicals and heavy metals.

EYES

As a general cleanser a quarter of a teaspoon of salt in a quarter of a pint of bottled water is an easily made solution. For a herbal eye-drop infusion Diane Stein recommends cineraria, rue, sage tea or celandine and the floral essences crab apple, camphor or hawthorn for cleansing. Cucumber juice is also very soothing for sore eyes.

If there are cataracts this condition can be due to nutritional deficiencies, in particular a lack of vitamin C, the B complex, vitamins A, D and E, selenium and zinc.

Richard Pitcairn advocates putting a drop of eucalyptus honey in eyes with cataracts twice a day for several weeks, and reports that this procedure has resulted in cataract reductions and cures.

Homoeopathically: *Calc Fluor* or *Natrum Mur 30c* may help with recently formed cataracts and *Silica 200c* is useful with established cataracts. *Ledum Palustre* or *Symphytum 30c* should be used when there are eye injuries and *Euphrasia Officinalis* diluted 1 in 20 parts water is good when there are scratches or superficial cuts.

Herbally: Cold chamomile tea is excellent for bathing sore eyes.

F is For:

FIGHTING

Homoeopathically: Tim Couzens and Grace McHatty suggest *Hyoscyamus* and *Anacardium*, Nick Thompson recommends *Lycopodium* for particularly aggressive cats who go looking for trouble and *Belladonna* for cats with a very quick and aggressive temper. Mark Elliott recommends *Staphysagria* for cats that are terrorising newcomers. *Lachesis* is an appropriate remedy for suspicious, jealous female cats, often vocal, who anger easily.

Herbally: Skullcap and valerian are the remedies for calming the animals.

FEAR

Homoeopathically there are several remedies: *Aconite, Arnica, Argentum Nitricum, Arsenicum Album, Gelsemium, Ignatia, Nux Vomica, Phosphorus, Pulsatilla* and *Stramonium*.

Aconite is recommended for cats whose fear turns to anger and may be due to pain. *Argentum Nitricum* and *Arsenicum Album* are good for cats who have a restless manner and seem rather anxious. *Gelsemium* is a useful remedy for very timid cats who are sometimes paralysed with fear and then hide away at any disturbance. *Ignatia* should be given when there is worry over the death of a fellow cat or owner and when the cat has suffered a particularly traumatic experience. *Nux Vomica* is appropriate for very nervous cats who often hate being handled but will fight aggressively if cornered. *Pulsatilla* is for shy, gentle cats, usually female, who like the protection of human company. *Stramonium* and *Arnica* should be given if a cat is distressed and unusually anxious about being handled, perhaps after a fright or an accident.

FLEAS

Fleas are an on-going battle. One doesn't want to be so heavy-handed with chemicals that the immune system is impaired, but at the same time one does not want the flea to take over and create an infestation as that will also cause disease. I do not believe in giving chemicals internally but brewers' yeast and garlic can be effective flea deterrents. The sugars in some commercial pet foods may also make an animal more attractive to fleas and they are particularly vulnerable if they have a weak immune system. It is therefore very important to feed pure foods – whether cooked or commercial – and to supplement with a good feline multi vitamin and mineral formula.

The main anti-flea herbs are eucalyptus, citronella, cedar, rosemary and fennel which can be pulverised and made into a flea powder. You can also make good herbal collars from herbal oils. Corpore Sano is a good anti-parasite shampoo. Juliette de Bairacli Levy also recommends her lemon skin tonic, which is made by putting a sliced lemon into almost boiling water. It should be left to cool overnight and then put on the coat of the cat in question and can be used on a daily basis as it is harmless. A flea comb is the other important piece of equipment as it picks up fleas as it moves through the fur and these can then be drowned in hot soapy water or popped between two thumb nails. If things cannot be controlled herbally then use a chemical spray or spot very sparingly and be on the alert for side effects and do NOT overdose on any account. Just as important as the products are regular vacuuming and washing of bedding – which should be picked up carefully so nothing falls out – to get rid of flea dirts and eggs. The bedding should be washed in hot water. Lavender can be left near the bedding as fleas dislike it.

Homoeopathically: *Sulphur* is excellent for skin and is also a possible flea deterrent. *Urtica* can be given if there is an allergy to flea collars. *Phos Tox* can also be very effective.

31

G is For:

GASTRITIS

Cats are much fussier eaters than dogs, but they can still get gastric problems by consuming the wrong foods. These can be things they have scavenged or even a sharp object which has been eaten accidentally. On one occasion a cat receiving acupuncture treatment swallowed an acupuncture needle when no one was looking! Normally such objects need to be removed surgically and a delay can prove fatal. Food allergies are frequently a problem and I find that my older cats (usually from the age of about thirteen) start to have an intolerance to the additives, colourants, preservatives and sugars in some commercial foods. A fast of twenty-four hours is often beneficial, followed by a complete change in diet to home-cooked foods such as chicken, pheasant, rabbit, turkey and pulses and rice, millet and grains. With gastritis stomach enzymes can also be helpful and you can give feline liquid vitamins if the animal is severely run down and its immune system needs building up. Worms can also bring on vomiting and diarrhoea so your cat should also be checked for these and given either a wormer for round worms (more common) or tape worms (less common but possible).

Homoeopathically: *Morgan Gaertner* worked very well on Cardy, my white Cornish Rex, who suffered from intestinal disorders for some time. Other remedies are: *Nux Vomica* for serious cases accompanied by thirst; *Ipecac* for frequent sickness, *Phosphorus* if there is vomiting with pain, *Camphora* if the cause is salmonella, *Arsenicum Album* when the food is questionable, *Pulsatilla* should be given when your pet is wanting your attention and drinks in an unfamiliar way. *Hypericum* is useful when there is pain.

Herbally: Slippery elm, dandelion, peppermint and camomile are good digestive herbs, as is Berberis.

GRIEF

Can cats grieve? The answer is yes, they definitely can. My cats Blackie and Whitey were inseparable and when the latter was run over by a car on a country lane Blackie was quite bereft. Whitey had been his little friend's protector, caring for him and curling up with him in a chair each night. Blackie cried so piteously as he went around looking for him day after day that we decided to get him another companion. The arrival of the newcomer, Coley, gave him something to think about. However, although they tolerated each other they behaved as acquaintances rather than friends. It wasn't until the arrival of Rexy, the Black Cornish Rex, that Blackie found true feline friendship once more.

Nutritionally, vitamin Bs are said to aid depression (in humans as well) so brewers' yeast, which contains vitamin B, can be given. However if your pet is allergic to yeast a 10 mg vitamin B complex can be sprinkled on food or pushed down the throat after feeding.

Homoeopathically: *Ignatia* is the main remedy for grief. *Nat Mur* can be given after *Ignatia* particularly if the animal seems to want to be left alone. *Nux Vom* is also possible for a cat that does not want to be handled; however, if the reverse is true and your pet craves attention, *Pulsatilla* may be more appropriate. *Staphisagria* is good for grief when it is accompanied by symptoms such as hair loss. *Aurum* is appropriate when there is a deep depression and *Causticum* works well when the animal appears to age after losing a companion, either animal or human, that has probably had a worrying illness over a long period.

Herbally: Camomile, skullcap and valerian are very calming. Flower remedies Honeysuckle or Star of Bethlehem may be given to animals when they have lost their owner or fellow cat. Olive can be helpful when the worry has been long-standing.

H is For:

HEART

Heart problems are fairly common in older cats. There are excellent conventional veterinary drugs available, but there are also a number of things that can be done at home. The first thing is to make the animal lose any unnecessary weight by a) putting it on a very pure diet which is sugar and salt free and cutting out 'treats' and b) trying to stop it being a couch potato by encouraging it to exercise a little more, whether with toys inside or more time spent outside.

Nutritionally, vitamins E, A and D are very important as are chromium, selenium, zinc and a B complex vitamin. An all-in-one feline multi vitamin, multi mineral would be a minimum requirement and in an older cat I would definitely boost the vitamin C daily intake to 500 mg. If the cat is taking heart tablets it may need to take extra potassium which could be depleted by the drugs.

Homoeopathically: *Spongia Tosta* may be useful particularly when there is a cough. *Calc Fluor* is good for a weakened heart muscle. *Crataegus Oxycantha* may help if there is fluid retention and Mark Elliott sometimes suggests a *Cactus* mix.

Herbally: Juliette de Bairacli Levy makes a rosemary and honey tea for cats with heart problems. Skullcap is calming and alfalfa or Yarrow helps with blood pressure, while dandelion leaf acts as a diuretic.

HYGIENE

Cats are very clean animals but in a domestic situation they need a bit of help. However, do beware of strong chemicals which have an adverse effect on the sensitive metabolisms of felines and use biodegradable products. You will need to keep their bedding clean on a regular basis to get rid of flea eggs and to vacuum the surrounding area. If cats eat rotten food they can easily succumb to gastritis. Their food bowls should be washed daily in water and a biodegradable washing liquid. Indoor cat litter should be cleaned at least twice a day and the litter disposed of hygienically. Your cat, especially if it is long-haired, will need help with its grooming, and brushing daily will remove excess knots and excess hair that could cause fur balls. A flea comb is most important to catch the flea population and in the height of summer you may need a herbal flea collar or a small amount of spray. Your cat should keep itself reasonably clean, but if you live in the centre of a city where there are more toxic substances, or if your cat falls into something, then a biodegradable shampoo is in order.

HEALING

Cats can respond very well to the laying on of hands by a genuine healer. A troubled or nervous cat can often become so calm under a healer's hands that it actually falls asleep. If an animal is fatally ill a healer can also be a very beneficial soothing presence. Most holistic vets will be able to recommend an animal healer.

I is For:

INSECT BITES

If your cat is severely stung by bees or wasps you should take it to your vet as there may be an allergic reaction. Internally, *Apis Mel* or *Ledum Palustre* may be appropriate. Externally you can try and remove the sting with tweezers and then rub the area with *Urtica Urens* in liquid form. If the sting should become septic *Chininum Sulphuricum* and the herb echinacea may be helpful. A raw onion or garlic can take the smarting out of an insect bite if it is put on the spot gently.

IMMUNE SYSTEM

It is when the immune system is under par that cats, like humans, become prone to ailments and diseases. Correct nutrition is the key to a healthy feline immune system with the correct balance of taurine, vitamins, minerals, anti-oxidants and essential oils. If you are feeding pure organic foods, either raw or lightly cooked, there should be little need for supplements; but if you are feeding cheap commercial foods your cat may need supplements. The other thing that can harm the immune system is over-vaccination. Some vets are now saying that vaccinating at three yearly intervals may be sufficient, as antibodies from the previous vaccination can still be giving protection over that time span. Homoeopathic nosodes from a holistic vet can also be a healthy alternative to vaccination. However, in case of serious illness when conventional veterinary medicine has not made any headway, I have had enormous success in keeping my cats healthy by boosting their immune system. Vitamin C 500–1000 mg daily (depending on the size of the cat) stomach enzymes, organic garlic and feline anti-oxidants, essential oils, vitamins and minerals (either in powder or liquid form depending on the digestive system) and echinacea are a daily requirement for any cat of mine with a health problem. However, I am pleased to say that as they are given supplements regularly my vets' bills tend to be very small and infrequent.

J is For:

Jealousy

Jealousy can be a major problem in cats and sometimes the cat will spray, fight, and at worst, it may even leave home. The jealousy is not necessarily always triggered off by another cat, as often the cat is treated like the baby of the family until a real baby comes along. If it is then excluded it will naturally become upset and stressed and, if it can find alternative accommodation with friendly neighbours, may even leave home.

The feelings of jealousy occur particularly at the introduction of a new feline, especially if it is an adult cat. If you are getting two new cats it is very important that they are both introduced to your home on the same day. That way there should be no territorial disputes as neither can claim prior ownership.

If you have two cats and one dies do not presume that your old cat will like a newcomer. It will have had a particular relationship with your old cat which is not necessarily replaceable. Some breeders introduce a new cat in a large cage to old cats so that its smell can mingle with the existing cat scents. When it is let out the cats may accept it as its smell seems familiar. When I introduce a new cat I restrict it to one small room at first, before giving it the run of the rest of the house and the other cats. It then has a territory which is its own and serves as a bolt hole if it feels the need to get away from the other animals.

If you are replacing a cat and still have another it is normally best to get either one or two kittens, but they must not be left alone together until you are certain that they have been accepted. If you have a geriatric cat it may be better to introduce two kittens as they can take their energy out on each other rather than the old cat. However, there are occasions when the old cat (often a

Burmese or Siamese type feline) will not accept the new kitten or cat at any level. In that case you will have to give up and re-home the newcomer. However, before you do that there are some homoeopathic and herbal remedies which can be tried.

Homoeopathically: My friend Mrs Cross used *Staphysagria* on her jealous female who started to spray badly when a new kitten was introduced. *Lachesis* is appropriate for a jealous nature and *Arsenicum Album* can be used when the cat is particularly possessive.

Herbally: Tim Couzens and Grace McHatty recommend flower remedies: a) holly for cats that are possessive, hate and are jealous b) beech for cats who respond badly to change, in particular the introduction of a new cat or baby to the household and c) chicory for egotistic, possessive, selfish felines who find it hard to share their owners. They also suggest that the aromatherapy oils jasmine, ylang ylang and grapefruit may have a role to play with different kinds of jealous cats.

K is For:

KITTENS

Kittens are the most enchanting creatures but if you want one – or two – please contact your local pet rescue centre first. They cannot cope with the vast numbers of unwanted kittens and will be grateful for your call. You will find a huge variety: long-hairs, short-hairs, grey, ginger, tabby, tortoiseshell, black or white, extrovert or shy, talkative or quiet and they all need loving homes.

Cats, like people, have different personalities and I have come across instances where a cat and a person have not got on. One was a white cat I rescued who didn't like ME. Fortunately – so far – it is the only time it has happened but I was most offended! She now lives most happily with the journalist Moira Petty whom she adores. Another cat, a black and white Cornish Rex called Harriet, ran away from home twice because she couldn't stand her owner. She is now blissfully happy with my friend Wendy Gaye. Therefore do make sure the cat takes to you and you take to it

before giving it a home. Another friend, Gladys Roberts, adopts animals who are physically imperfect. If you have a kind heart please don't go for the most beautiful kittens that will find homes easily, but also consider the less fortunate, physically imperfect ones who often seem more grateful too.

Before getting a kitten do consider your circumstances. Are you on a main road? Do you live in a small flat? Are you out at work all day? If so you would be far better off with an older cat. A kitten is not traffic-wise, a tiny flat may not give a kitten the room it needs to expend its energy, and if you are out all day a single kitten may well get bored and depressed. If you are away in the daytime two kittens would be a better option as they would keep each other company. Before you bring your kitten(s) home you will need to invest in a cat litter tray and cat litter, a flea comb, some cat biscuit and some kitten food. There aren't very many on the market but I prefer Denes (no additives, colourants, preservatives or sugars) or Whiskas or Felix kitten foods. I feed three times a day up to six months, then twice a day thereafter, I also keep handy vitamin C powder and stomach enzymes and feline vitamins, oils, and minerals, which you can give at the first sign of a cough or sneeze. However, personally I alternate supplements in my cat's food on a regular basis so I am sure they are all getting optimum nutrition.

Some vets suggest you vaccinate at about eight weeks, but I prefer to keep kittens of mine inside and vaccinate at fourteen weeks when their immune system is stronger. After the first two shots I then vaccinate my cats every three years, and if the cat has any health problems at all I won't dare vaccinate in case the shot triggers off something serious.

If you live in an area where there may be hazards outside like large tomcats, dogs or foxes, only let a small cat outside under supervision or wait until it is large and smart enough to protect itself. It is also imperative to familiarise your cat with its new territory so that it knows the safe areas it can flee to should it be pursued.

Most important of all, do handle and play with your kitten. If it has had a bad experience it may take a little more time and patience but I have always found facilitating the transition from a scared timid kitten to a trusting, affectionate, purring cat to be a most rewarding experience.

L is For:

LEUKAEMIA (FeLV)

As this disease can have various symptoms, for a proper diagnosis consult a holistic vet. A cat with feline leukaemia can spread the disease to other cats, however the illness need not be fatal and some can recover from it, particularly with the help of nutritional, homoeopathic and herbal supplements.

The disease may have been triggered by vaccination if the cat had an impaired immune system, and once it has had the disease it should NEVER be vaccinated for anything again. One of the problems with recovery may be that the cat goes off its food. If so, one should force feed, particularly with liquid vitamins and vitamin C crystals dissolved in pure water in syringes. Mushy organic chicken (organic chicken breast blended with spring water against dehydration) with a little diced chicken liver is also excellent to get an invalid eating again. However, try anything which may get it feeding.

Nutritionally: Give large doses daily of vitamin C 500–1000 mg (depending on the size of the cat) also a B vitamin complex 20 mg, half a teaspoon of cod liver oil, 100 iu of vitamin E, 15 mg of zinc, 10 mg of Coenzyme Q10 and a feline liquid multi vitamin–multi mineral supplement. The best foods for optimum nutrition are: organic oats, broccoli, turkey, chicken, liver, free range egg yolk, alfalfa, garlic and kelp with calcium powder. (Garlic should not be given at the same meal as vitamins which should be taken either with or after food. The exception is zinc, which should be given on its own, preferably at night).

Homoeopathically: George MacLeod recommends a nosode of FeLV blood or a nosode of *Lymphosarcoma* tumour. *Nux Vomica*, Magnesium, *Calcarea Fluorica*, *Silicea*, *Pulsatilla*, *Phosphorus*, *Sepia* or *Nitricum Acidum* are remedies which may help. Pitcairn also recommends *Nat Mur* for a weak cat with severe dehydration and anaemia (one tablet three times daily) and separately, *Calc Phos* (one tablet a day).

Herbally: Liquid echinacea could help, and Anita Frazier recommends pansy and McCartney rose flower essences.

You must consult a holistic vet as steroids, cortisone and X-rays may not be helpful and vaccinations could be damaging. Food should be organic when possible and you should use only herbal products, avoiding all chemicals.

LIVER

The liver is one of the most important organs in the body and a healthy liver is crucial to the well-being of a cat. Signs of liver problems usually include pale stools, sickness, diarrhoea and a refusal of food. If the whites of the eyes are yellow the cat probably has jaundice. Severe liver disease may mean dark stools accompanied by blood.

The first thing to do is to abstain from giving food for twenty-four hours, administering liquids only. After that it is imperative to feed very pure, organic, non-fat meals. You should give lean cooked chicken or turkey, free range egg yolks, with a little porridge (oats) and grated raw green vegetables such as broccoli. A little beetroot, parsley, garlic, dandelion or milk thistle may also be helpful.

Vitamin C 500–1000 mg (depending upon the size of the cat), Coenzyme Q10 10 mg, cod liver oil (quarter of a teaspoon), digestive enzymes and aloe vera could all be beneficial.

Homoeopathically: George MacLeod recommends *Phosphorus* if the stools are clay coloured and *Chelidonium* if the faeces are golden yellow. He suggests *Lycopodium* for more chronic cases, *Berberis* if there is loin weakness with pungent urine and *Chionanthus* for jaundice with putty-like stools. For cirrhosis when there is constipation, sickness and fluid in the stomach he recommends (apart from *Phosphorus*, *Lycopodium* and *Berberis*) *Carduus Mar* which is known to be good for this condition, and *Ptelea* which may act like a drainage remedy.

Herbally: Give dandelion, berberis or milkthistle.

Sunshine may also be helpful to a cat with impaired liver function.

M is for:

MATERNITY

Much as I love kittens I know I can take any number from my local cat rescue, so I have never felt the need to breed from my own cats. I have therefore correlated most of my information on maternity from my friend Paddy Cutts' book *The Complete Cat Book*. Apparently a female cat is named after the old word *quean*, meaning a whore or a hussy, and when you hear one calling and see their physical stance you can appreciate why!

The first thing about mating a queen is that she should be a) Over one year old and b) Very healthy. Any calcium deficiency could mean her kittens will be born with skeletal abnormalities and she herself could go down with eclampsia which might prove fatal. A female should be mated on the second or third day of her call, and as soon as you notice that she is pregnant she should be put on a healthy diet along with feline vitamin and mineral supplements.

The average gestation period, give or take a couple of days, is sixty-five days. A few days before the birth the queen will probably want to make a nest somewhere dark and quiet so you can help by providing a cardboard box full of cotton fabric and newspaper. If you supply numerous layers you can remove pieces as they become soiled.

Most pregnancies are simple but you need to have clean towels, a kitchen roll, blunt topped scissors and a bowl of boiled water handy. These might be needed if the queen omits to bite through the kitten's umbilical cord, which you then have to cut one and a half inches from the kitten. You need to squeeze the cord to stem the blood flow and help clotting and the kitten should be rubbed vigorously. The placenta is usually eaten by the mother. The birth may last an hour or half a day. Obviously, if there is any real problem and a kitten is stuck a vet should be called.

Homoeopathically: *Pulsatilla* or *Caulophyllum*.

Herbally: Raspberry leaf may help around the fifth week of pregnancy until a week after the kittens are born. It is thought to prevent miscarriages and encourages lactation. Bach Rescue Remedy is always good in an emergency.

MINERALS

People often talk about vitamins but not everybody realises that minerals have just as important a role to play in maintaining a healthy immune system. Many years ago there were lots of trace minerals (over seventy) in our soil which were absorbed by plants and then passed into the food chain. However, since the advent of chemicals, including organo-phosphates, and since the soil has been overworked over a long period of time, all the minerals which are so essential to our health are now virtually non-existent and our food supply is seriously deficient in minerals. Every part of the body requires minerals and without them not only we, but our animals too, will have serious health problems. It was because I couldn't find a multi mineral product for cats that my vet formulated the Feline Care mineral supplement.

MOPING

Cats can very definitely mope. They can mope at a change of abode, a change of owner, the introduction of a new person or animal into the household and the loss of either a person or an animal from their immediate family.

Homoeopathically: Tim Couzens recommends *Arsenicum Album* for despair.

Bach Flower Remedies: Tim Couzens recommends gorse (*Ulex Europaeus*) for animals that seem to have given up the will to live, often with severe health problems. He also recommends olive when a cat is exhausted after a period of stress.

Aromatherapy: Nelly Grosjean suggests basil and sweet marjoram for depression. Aromatherapy oils should NEVER be put on a cat's skin or fur, but should be inhaled at a distance of at least one foot.

N is For:

NERVES

Cats love routine, consistency and being in one place. You can get a young cat used to commuting between different places, but an older one will undergo stress if moved. I always thought Hodge, my talking Tonkinese, was a 'person' cat as he and I had such a loving relationship. However, when he was first ill I took him from our farmhouse where he lived to London for another veterinary opinion. I thought he would enjoy my exclusive company at our flat without the other animals, but not at all – he wanted to be on his home territory and howled so loudly that the neighbours complained. Needless to say immediately after the visit to the vet's we headed back to our Chichester home!

Kittens and cats from rescue centres have invariably had a stressful time and should be treated with TLC (tender loving care). Coley had been rescued by my friend Min Flower after yobs had shot darts into him. As a result he had a feisty personality: 'bomb proof' was how Min described him, and he certainly lived up to that description as he eradicated all the vermin and even scared our Dobermann Pinschers, who developed a healthy respect for him! Alfie, my seven-month-old kitten, had a very similar start in life to Coley and very much resembles him in personality. No two cats are ever identical, but with Alfie around there is never a day that I am not reminded of dear Coley.

Cats are ultra-sensitive and can be subject to depression as a result of some tragedy in their lives and unless something is done to snap them out of it they can give up and die. I certainly felt there was that possibility with both Alfie and Duchess, the white moggie I took in. It was only by lavishing a great deal of time and attention on them, combined with giving them very pure foods and immune system building nutritional supplements, that they pulled through.

Foods that are calming include oats, barley and turkey with sufficient calcium, along with feline minerals and vitamins A, D, E, C 500–1000 mg, and the mineral zinc 15 mg. B complex vitamins are said to be good for depression.

Homoeopathically: *St John's Wort* (hypericum) helps depression and Francis Hunter recommends *Scuttelaria* (skullcap) twice a day for a week for depressed animals. Dr Richard Pitcairn recommends *Kali Phos* for nervous animals. *Ignatia* is excellent for grieving animals and *Arsenicum Album* can help animals who are panicking.

Herbally: Vervain may aid depression and camomile, hops and valerian are calming.

Aromatherapy: According to Nelly Grosjean lavender and sweet marjoram can help traumatised cats.

NEUTERING

Tomcats are the scourge of any neighbourhood, so if you want to be popular with your neighbours I recommend that you have your male kitten neutered at six to eight months. Tomcats are aggressive, they beat up other cats and often enter cat flaps and spray their obnoxious smelling urine around people's houses to mark their territory.

The other important factor to remember is that they will roam for miles to find an unspayed female and will then contribute to the thousands of unwanted cats mouldering away in rescue centres. There is no doubt that a responsible cat owner is one that will have his or her cat neutered or spayed. The stench of tomcat urine is very difficult to remove – it can take years – so it is important to neuter the cat early before it develops the habit of spraying. None of the cats I have had neutered at an early age – before nine months – have ever sprayed. It is only those older cats that I have rescued, like Hodge at six and Cardy at ten, that were manic sprayers. So if you want an affectionate, gentle male, that is unlikely to fight, stays close to home and doesn't make your home stink of cat's pee you should have your animal snipped.

The neutering operation is very simple, but for any surgery I always ask for the best anaesthetic in case of an allergic reaction. To boost the immune system you can administer A, E, C and B complex vitamins and zinc before and after surgery. Vitamin E oil can be beneficial if scar tissue is itching. With all the cats I have had neutered, I have to say there has never been the slightest problem other than a little wooziness, post surgery, on the day of the operation. When Alfie, my fiendish long-haired orphan kitten, was 'done' recently at seven months his personality improved immeasurably. He is now very affectionate and has stopped terrorising all the other cats!

Homoeopathically: After any operation you can give *Arnica, Hypericum* or *Phosphorus. Staphysagria* for 'surgical and mental' insult.

Herbally: Echinacea liquid can be used, along with Bachs Rescue Remedy. On any post operation tissue you can use calendula.

NUTRITION

The basic dietary requirements are what foods to give, how much and how often. The best food to give is raw food (if it comes from a reliable, unconditional source) or home-cooked food. However, cooking depletes taurine, vitamins and minerals so feline supplements may be added when the food has cooled down, along with calcium or powdered eggshell. Ideal proteins for cats can be found in chicken, turkey, guinea fowl, pheasant, rabbit, liver (in small amounts not more than twice a week) lamb (but not for arthritic cats), cod, halibut, skate, haddock, coley, plaice, bream, mackerel, pilchards, salmon and herring. Protein for vegetarian felines are abundant in pulses, seeds and nuts (not peanuts), free range eggs, goats' milk and goats' yoghurt and a calcium and taurine supplement may be added. However, cats can have allergies to dairy products, and other foods like carrots (they cannot synthesise beta carotene), tuna (it depletes their vitamin E), beef, yeast, corn, soya and even chicken can cause problems. Good vegetables to give are broccoli, brussels sprouts, cabbage, peas, beans, pumpkin and beetroot. A pinch of thyme, rosemary or garlic can be a healthy flavoursome addition. For carbohydrates one can add millet, oats, rice, spelt and polenta (corn meal). Organic or free range products are preferable, particularly for cats with serious health problems. If you are feeding commercial foods you may find it a false economy to buy cheap cans which may contain a lot of moisture. Cat food like Hills, Eukanuba, Naturediet, Hi-Life and Denes are more expensive, but I find my cats eat less because they are packed full of goodness.

How much should one give and how often? Based on my experience with the numerous cats I have I would never give even a big cat more than one large can a day. Personally I don't like to feed just cereal nuggets, but I might give a very small handful of biscuit as a treat mid-day or late at night and always make sure there is plenty of fresh water near at hand to prevent dehydration.

In terms of home-cooked food I would feed kittens 70 per cent protein with 30 per cent grains and vegetables; and adult cats 60 per cent protein with 40 per cent grains and vegetables. I would feed: a kitten of three weeks every four hours and not more than six tablespoons per day; a kitten of eight weeks four tablespoons three times a day and a five-pound kitten of four months about one cup per day. For an eight-pound pregnant queen I would feed about one and a half cups per day, a small adult cat about half to three quarters of a cup daily and a large adult cat one, to one and a half cups daily.

However, for optimum nutrition, with home-cooking I always add taurine, calcium (this can be bonemeal or crushed eggshell), rotating the vitamins, minerals, essential oils and anti-oxidants and varying the menus. That way you can be sure your cats are getting everything they need to be healthy felines.

O Is For:

OBESITY

An obese cat is a potentially unhealthy cat so if your cat is fat you would be well advised to put it on a diet. The first thing to do is to see whether the commercial food you may be feeding contains either 'sugars' or 'caramels' in the small print. If it does switch to one that doesn't, like Denes or Naturediet. The second thing is not to overfeed, as in the wild cats would simply catch a mouse, vole or small bird from time to time. It is unlikely that they would sit down to a huge meal twice a day, so put down food and if it is not eaten remove it or keep it in the refrigerator for one more serving.

When I rescued two overweight cats from an elderly lady who was spoiling them with food in a tiny flat packed with furniture so they could hardly move I put them on the following diet: skinned turkey or chicken with occasional liver plus rice and oatbran (for bulk), green vegetables and a supplement of feline vitamins and minerals to boost the immune system. All treats should be eliminated and the cat should be encouraged to exercise.

ORPHANS

It is very hard to perform all the functions that a mother cat does for her kittens. She keeps them warm with her body, she cleans and stimulates them with her tongue and she feeds them with her milk which, if the queen has been vaccinated, will give her kittens antibodies against disease until they are fit enough to have vaccinations themselves.

For warmth you can give a covered hot water bottle (reheated regularly), a microwave heat pad, or an electric pad set low (with a circuit breaker for safety) or a plastic bed with a heater inside it on which you can put a towel or bedding. Young kittens lose body heat very easily so they must be kept warm.

The choice of cat litter is very important for orphaned kittens with no mother to guide or clean them. It should be biodegradable, and wood or paper-based so as not to be toxic if ingested. 'Clumping' formulas are not desirable at this stage, as their legs are so tiny the litter can actually clump on a damp kitten. For grooming, I only use a flea comb on tiny kittens, or moist cotton wool

pollyanna pickering

on particularly dirty areas. I would not want to bathe a kitten in case it got chilled. However if the kitten fell into a toxic substance one would, of course, wash it and dry it thoroughly afterwards. It is difficult feeding orphaned kittens as nothing is as good as mother's milk but when they are very tiny you can use small droppers or syringes to feed them. Some vets recommend commercial formula milk for tiny kittens, but my local Cat and Rabbit Rescue and I advocate goats' milk as the most acceptable food for the very young. When they are first born they require feeding approximately every two hours, day and night, so it is very tiring work indeed. By the age of three weeks Sidlesham Cat and Rabbit Rescue introduce a commercial kitten food and sometimes freshly cooked chicken. As the ones I rescued were particularly delicate I mixed breast of chicken with a dessert spoon of bottled water (against dehydration) together with feline liquid vitamins in a child's blender. At the age of three weeks I was able to feed them every four hours so life was slightly less frantic. By the time they were re-homed at the age of twelve weeks they were being fed three times a day. By then they could also eat Denes, Whiskas or Felix kitten food, besides home-cooking, which made things easier for the new owners.

P is For:

PERITONITIS

(FIP-Feline Infectious Peritonitis)

Having experienced this disease first-hand with Byron, the British Short-Haired Tip that I took on at the age of ten, I can mercifully say that the outlook need not be as gloomy as some vets or indeed some books would suggest. However, what I did find out was that antibiotics – Byron had three courses of different ones – were not the answer, as after each course the disease returned.

Byron had the illness particularly badly as he had fluid on the lungs and a distended abdomen as well. However, with my 'nothing to lose' philosophy when dealing with a particularly fatal disease I reached for every alternative medicine at my disposal in liquid, powder, capsule, tablet and syringe form with food or in water. This is what l gave him: Nutritionally: Home-cooked food consisting predominantly of chicken, turkey, or rabbit with a little rice, broccoli, cabbage and beetroot with chicken liver twice a week.

For Byron, who was a large cat, I gave after food:

1) Vitamin C 500 mg twice daily.
2) Vitamin E 50 iu once a day.
3) Cod liver oil, half a teaspoon daily.
4) Zinc 15 mg (taken separately).
5) Kelp.
6) B complex 50 mg daily.
7) Digestive enzymes, half a teaspoon (kept in the fridge).
8) Selenium 50 mg.
9) For anaemia I gave a liquid supplement by either Feline Care or Floradix (kept in the fridge).

Homoeopathically: *Cantharis, Carduus Mar, Lycopodium, Mercurius Sulphuricus, Tub Bov* or *Arsenicum Album* may be appropriate.

Herbally: Slippery elm, nettles, echinacea and organic garlic.

According to Richard Pitcairn the FIP virus can sometimes be triggered by the Feline Leukaemia vaccination. A flea infestation would certainly not help the condition either, as it could cause anaemia.

POISONING

Potential dangers are everywhere but the most common cause of poisoning seems to be lawn weedkiller. I have come across it twice and in both instances the cats died, so try not to use toxic weed-killers yourself and ask your neighbours to let you know when they are spraying so you can keep your pet in. Other harmful poisons include certain disinfectants and some plants, as well as woodworm and dry rot treatments. A number of decorative house-plants are a problem, while other hazards are found in insecti-cides, antifreeze (which is sweet to drink) rubber bands, bits of string and electric cables. If you need to induce vomiting you can place salt on the back of the tongue.

Homoeopathically: you can give *Nux Vom* or for particularly toxic substances, *Arsenicum Album.*

Herbally: Slippery elm and aloe vera may be helpful.

Q is For:

QUEENS

If you are going to breed from your cat remember all the unwanted felines in the world – and that rearing kittens properly is more expensive than actually investing in a spaying operation. The poor pregnant queens that end up in rescue centres are often in a dreadful state, flea ridden, undernourished and emaciated. They give birth to wormy, undersized kittens, sometimes with abnormalities or with such poor immune systems that they lose the fight for survival. What a depressing business it is too. I lost three out of five kittens that were in a perilous state at three weeks, though fortunately the remaining two, after a lot of hard work, are now healthy adolescents. Duchess and her four kittens were very sick indeed when I took them on and Negra and her four offspring were undersized and emaciated.

So if you insist on breeding your queen she should be fed with the very best of pure foods, particularly those high in protein. Crushed eggshell or a calcium supplement are most important, as are vitamin C (500–1000 mg), brewers' yeast or a B complex (30 mg), vitamin E (50–100 iu), kelp and a feline multi mineral which should be given daily. One teaspoon of extra virgin olive oil should be added to food and a quarter of a teaspoon of cod liver oil should be given three times a week. Chicken or lambs' liver should also be cooked twice a week.

Watch out for a condition called ECLAMPSIA at the end of or after pregnancy which occurs because of a lack of calcium (the kittens take a great deal of calcium from their mother's body). Usually the symptoms are violent trembling, but there may also be a high fever accompanied by loss of appetite. To prevent this you should make sure the pregnant queen has enough calcium.

Homoeopathically: *Viburnum* can be useful in early pregnancy to prevent miscarrying. If there is haemorrhaging give either *Arnica* or *Ipecac*. For calcium deficiency/depletion you can give *Belladonna* *6c* every fifteen minutes, but you should see a holistic veterinarian as soon as possible for calcium injections to prevent eclampsia.

Herbally: Raspberry leaf is renowned for its help throughout pregnancy. Bach Rescue Remedy can help if the queen is distressed while giving birth.

R is For:

RENAL FAILURE

Renal or kidney failure is something I learnt about to my cost as my lovely black and white moggie, Coley, died from it at the age of thirteen. He had been a dry biscuit addict, which may well have exacerbated the problem, and had been frequently vomiting, which can be a sign of kidney problems. As the disease progressed he started to drink large amounts of water (having been a poor drinker previously) and to urinate frequently. Unfortunately by the time I noticed these changes and went to my conventional vet (this was before I knew of the existence of holistic vets) I was told that there was no hope and poor Coley died.

One always tends to blame oneself if a cat dies early, and compared with my other seventeen-year-old cats Coley died in middle age. Had I known the signs and had I known then what I know now there are things that I could have done for him which might well have prolonged his life. I did not, for instance, know about the colourants, additives, sugars and preservatives in some of the commercial foods as I never bothered to read the small print. I also did not know that dried foods may cause dehydration and kidney problems in cats that drink too little. What I should have done is cooked a little protein, such as chicken or turkey, with some white rice and broccoli, given taurine, a vitamin B complex (10 mg) vitamin C 500–1000 mg (depending on the size of the cat) vitamin A (1000 iu daily) and calcium (250 mg daily) possibly in crushed eggshell form. A little barley water or cranberry juice, one part to three parts water, could also have been given.

Homoeopathically: *Nux Vomica* helps with toxicity and sickness and *Nat Mur* may be appropriate if the cat is showing signs of thirst.

Herbally: Alfalfa tablets can be given with food.

If you do not have time to cook you may find there is a specially prepared food for kidney problems available from your vet's.

RINGWORM

Ringworm is an uncommon problem but it should be dealt with quickly as it can spread to other animals and people (I caught it from a kitten I befriended in Morocco). It is, in fact, a fungus not a worm and grows in the shape of a circle, infecting the hair and skin in that area.

Homoeopathically: *Sulphur* should be given internally. *Sepia* and Bacillinum are good.

Herbally: Richard Pitcairn recommends a brew of Plantago Major or an infusion of Hydrastis Canadiensis, which can be rubbed in twice a day.

If the problem persists consult a holistic vet.

S is For:

SKIN

Nutrition is the key to good skin so a healthy colourant-additive-sugar-preservative-free diet should be maintained. Dairy products can also cause skin allergies. If there are skin problems the main vitamins that help are C, E, A, B vitamins, and zinc, garlic and kelp should also be given. Vitamin E can also be rubbed directly on to bald patches.

Homoeopathically: *Sulphur* is the main remedy. *Calendula* in liquid form can help externally.

Herbally: Aloe vera and echinacea can be given internally and externally. Liquid honey can also be dabbed on a particularly bad area and calamine and witch hazel can be soothing.

Remember that a skin problem can also be due to fleas, or a flea allergy, so this should be treated accordingly.

SPAYING

I recently agreed to take in a lovely nine-month-old Devon Rex called Esmeralda. Apart from being riddled with fleas, we discovered she was pregnant. This was obviously why she had been jettisoned by her uncaring owner. A female should be spayed at the age of six months, and even then you should be alert for signs of an early heat. If she comes on heat it is not a disaster as she can be spayed in season. When I was looking after Duchess and Negra and their kittens I had them spayed when their kittens were eight weeks old, as they could have come on heat again from six weeks after giving birth. Some queens can become pregnant again a mere three weeks later. There are several other good reasons for spaying: 1) You will not attract tomcats to your area. 2) A cat that is bred too often will become debilitated (one of my cats was emaciated from over-breeding when I took her in from a breeder). 3) The cat will be protected from pyometria and their chances of getting breast cancer may be reduced.

With the over-population of felines and the euthanasia of so many unwanted pets do you want your cat's offspring to contribute to those numbers? Your cat could be responsible for thousands of unwanted felines in just a few years. It is also cheaper to spay your cat than to pay for the cost of building up the mother cat and feeding her kittens over eight weeks, not to mention the cost of worming and possible veterinary bills. Spaying is by far the cheapest – and kindest – option.

SPRAYING

Spraying is usually brought on by some form of disruption to a cat's life, like the introduction of a new cat to the household. Hodge, my Tonkinese, sprayed at the introduction of any new object and Cardy, my white Cornish Rex, had a spraying problem around other cats, as he had been a stud cat for many years. Normally, however, if cats like each other and are confident, spraying is not a problem as they do not feel the need to mark their territory. Fortunately, there are some homoeopathic remedies which may help.

Homoeopathically: *Staphysagria* was recommended by my vet for a friend's cat who took against the arrival of a new youngster and she found that the remedy cured the problem. Tim Couzens recommends *Ustilago* (apart from *Staphysagria*) and *Folliculinum*, *Oestrogen* and *Testosterone* which are produced from potentised hormones and may improve behaviour.

Herbally: Tim Couzens advocates flower remedies willow and walnut, which can be used together, and chicory, heather, larch or mimulus may also be appropriate.

SURGERY

Before an operation give *Arnica* and C, E and B vitamins, and minerals to boost the immune system. A cat should be starved for at least twelve hours before an operation. After surgery continue to give C, E and B vitamins and minerals, along with pure foods to quicken the recovery and to speed up healing. Rub either *Arnica* or calendula creams on the scar. If the cat scratches at the wound it may be necessary to get a collar (the shape of a lampshade) from the vet to prevent it reaching the affected area.

T is For:

TEETH

If you want your cat to have good teeth the first thing is to avoid sugary commercial foods. Nutritionally calcium and phosphorus in food are important for tooth development and vitamins and minerals help maintain healthy gums. Small raw bones (from a non-salmonella source) or some dry biscuit can aid in cleaning teeth, as indeed can a toothbrush.

Homoeopathically: *Calc Fluor* is the appropriate remedy.

Herbally: Myrrh and echinacea in liquid form make a good mouthwash, although it may prove difficult to administer!

TOXOPLASMOSIS

Toxoplasmosis is a disease which humans can pick up from under-cooked or raw meats or from certain animals, including cats. However, a person or cat with a healthy immune system who is on a nutritionally sound diet and taking a multi vitamin-mineral supplement is less likely to have a problem. Toxoplasmosis can be passed on through the faeces of a cat carrying the disease, so gloves should be used in cleaning a cat litter tray. Pregnant women are more susceptible so they should be particularly careful. Remember not to give undercooked or raw meat (unless it is organic) to either your cat or yourself, as that is a likely source of contamination.

Homoeopathically: *Calc Fluor* or *Silicea* may help.

U is For:

URINARY INFECTIONS

Urinary infections usually become obvious when the cat has trouble urinating or passes blood. It may also start to pee in unfamiliar places and avoid its litter tray. Some vets suspect that urinary tract disease may be due to feeding dry commercial foods over a long period of time. It is advisable to stop immediately, and the cat should be given chicken, turkey or rabbit with green vegetables or, if necessary, a very pure additive, preservative, colourant and sugar free commercial brand.

Vitamins C (500–1000 mg), E (50 iu), a B complex (20 mg) without yeast and a quarter of a teaspoon of cod liver oil should be given daily. When the condition subsides a daily intake of a feline multi vitamin-mineral powder should be maintained, along with vitamin C (100 mg) and a quarter of a teaspoon of cod liver oil twice a week.

Homoeopathically: *Cantharis, Sasparilla, Urtica Urens, Pulsatilla* or *Nux Vomica* can alleviate the symptoms.

Herbally: Cranberry juice (diluted one part to three parts water) or barley water can help. Parsley is also a good diuretic.

Of course if your cat is in obvious distress and its condition has become acute you should see a vet as quickly as possible.

V is For:

VACCINATIONS

The most recent veterinary thinking is that antibodies from vaccinations stay in the system for up to three years, so annual vaccinations may be unnecessary. The main trouble is that boarding catteries demand a recent vaccination, but I believe that edict should be changed. If you have any doubts go to a homoeopathic vet and ask for the homoeopathic alternative. According to Richard Allport, the homoeopathic vet at the Natural Medicine Veterinary Centre, 'Most veterinary surgeons in conventional practice feel that the normal vaccinations are, on the whole, safe and effective; but the majority of homoeopathic vets have serious worries about the effect of conventional vaccines on the immune system.' He adds, 'There seems a strong possibility that conventional vaccines may be a factor in the development of chronic diseases such as eczema, colitis and auto-immune conditions.' Dr Bruce Fogle, the Canadian vet, reports that the American Small

Animal Veterinary Association suggests that enteritis and flu jabs should be given every three years. However, they say that if the cat is in a high risk area then it may be necessary to vaccinate yearly.

Once I knew Hodge had the FIV virus and Byron had FIP they never had another vaccination, as it was important not to disturb their fragile immune systems. Alfie, my young orphaned kitten, was not vaccinated until seven months when he finally got well after months of diarrhoea from a food allergy. According to my vet, fourteen weeks is early enough for the first vaccination, provided the kitten is not roaming about outside where there are other strange cats. Prior to that a kitten's immune system can still be very delicate, and if the mother has been recently vaccinated it will have antibodies from that vaccination in its blood for a time anyway. All animals should be in optimum condition before vaccinating.

VITAMINS

All too often there are inadequacies in a cat's diet. A feline multi vitamin with minerals is designed to fill the nutritional gap between modern diets and a cat's daily needs, promoting optimum health and longevity. A balanced formulation like the Feline Care vitamin and mineral supplement contains kelp and green barley to fulfil a cat's need for chlorophyll and iodine. It also contains digestive enzymes for optimum digestion. A good feline vitamin-mineral supplement is insurance that your cat is getting its necessary daily quota of healthy vitamins, especially if you are feeding some of the cheaper commercial brands.

W is For:

WORMING

Juliette de Bairacli Levy recommends herbal wormers in her book *The Complete Herbal Handbook for the Dog and Cat*. However, I have never had any adverse effects administering modern day veterinary-prescribed wormers to my cats, although I do not believe in worming unnecessarily.

If you see what looks like long (usually up to half an inch) pieces of rice stuck to your cat's rear end or in its faeces they may well prove to be segments of tapeworm that have broken away. The wormer that I prefer, and push down my cats' throats, is called Droncit, but I sometimes use a Panacur powder in food for more difficult cats. It is important to keep on top of the flea problem as, if your cat swallows fleas whilst grooming itself, this may start up a tapeworm again.

Practically all of the kittens I rescued last summer had a round worm problem. Two orphaned tabby kittens had very distended bellies, while Alfie vomited a lot and had diarrhoea, and Negra and her kittens were emaciated and also had diarrhoea. Very occasionally one of my cats has vomited up a whole worm a few inches long, and sometimes you can find the same size worms in a litter tray amongst the stools. My preferred feline wormer for round worm is Endorid, which is palatable and can be disguised in food.

Homoeopathically: For tapeworms you can give *Felix Mas* or *Merc Cor* (when the cat is passing blood in its faeces). For round worms give *Cina*, *Chenopodium* or *Natrum Phos*.

Herbally: Hawthorn may be helpful. Oat bran and garlic are not liked by worms and may help if mixed in with a nutritionally sound diet.

X is For:

X-RAY

X-rays are a valuable diagnostic aid, particularly with bone problems or digestive disorders which may be caused by an obstruction. If you are worried that your cat has been exposed to too much radiation give vitamin C (up to 1000 mg a day for a large cat), kelp, bioflavanoids and vitamin Bs.

XENOPHOBIA (Fear of Foreigners)

Homoeopathically: *Hyoscyamus* is used on ferals who are suspicious of people. *Lycopodium* is the appropriate remedy for domestic cats who hate most strangers.

Herbally: Bach Rescue Remedy may calm down a cat that is stressed by someone new and impatiens can be very calming.

Y is For:

YEAST

Certain animals have a yeast allergy, in which case foods such as bread and mushrooms should be avoided, although you can buy soda bread which is not made with yeast. Some people and some animals also have an allergy to the new DNA-altered wheat and may fare better with old-fashioned organic wheat. However, if your cat does not have a yeast allergy brewers' yeast, which felines often find very tasty, is a useful source of the B vitamins which are particularly good for the nervous system.

Z is For:

ZINC

Zinc is one of the most valuable minerals in boosting the immune system. An animal with skin or coat problems may well be deficient in zinc and should be given a zinc tablet internally, while a zinc ointment can be used externally. Zinc is a bactericide and can be used after surgery or on burns. Zinc ointment may make the immune system function properly. It should be given as a supplement in all the major feline illnesses including cancer. It is a mineral which should be taken separately from the others and does not need to be taken with food.

WHAT'S IN

- If you have a new cat or kitten do put on an elastic collar with a disc, including your address on it, for at least the first two weeks. At the end of a fortnight the cat should have become accustomed to and accepted its new home.
- You should have a cat litter tray indoors for the first fortnight and should keep the windows and exterior doors closed. It is during this time that the cat is most likely to go missing. In the wild a cat would never urinate or defecate in the same place. Fussy cats may therefore need two litter trays.
- When you want to train your cat to go outside, slowly, daily, move the litter tray towards the back door and finally outside

the door. To train a cat to use a cat flap, placing food on the other side is often the answer.

- Do get a scratching post; there are excellent ones available and they save the furniture. A sharp 'NO' can have an effect on most sensitive felines who are found damaging the fabric or carpet. You can also cut a cat's nails, but this should be done under expert supervision with proper nail clippers. Be sure not to cut the pink quick as the nail will bleed profusely and be very painful. Some of my friends use emery boards on cats' nails most effectively.

- If you are out at work all day do get either an elderly cat who will spend much of the day sleeping or two young kittens to keep each other company and wear each other out. I always try to keep cats in pairs, they love feline company and tend to check up on each other at regular intervals, thereby staying close to home.

- If your cat does go missing place advertisements in the local paper, in all the local shops, and on trees and inform the police and the local cat rescue centres. The best idea with modern technology is to get your vet to tattoo the ear or microchip the cat's identity into its neck. That way its ownership can never be in dispute and it can always be traced. The majority of absentees are, unfortunately, victims of road accidents. If a cat is happy at home only a tragedy will prevent it from returning. We also had a semi-feral cat up a tree for a day and a night, but finally got her down with a ladder, a fishing net and thick gloves!

- Most important of all do get your cat spayed or neutered. A tomcat is less likely to spray if he has been neutered. This is also why young toms should be castrated early – after six months – before they get into bad habits. Recently I heard from Mrs Pat Cross, who had taken in two Cornish Rexes for me. One had died and she had acquired another rescued cat whereupon the old cat started to spray around the house and terrorise the newcomer. Fortunately she went to Mark Elliott, my homoeopathic vet, who prescribed i) *Staphysagria* for the aggressor's resentment and ii) Bachs Rescue Remedy for the timid newcomer. The latest news is that there is a truce with no fights and, just as important, no spraying.

Hodge, my Tonkinese, used to resent the introduction of

anything new to his territory – briefcases, shopping bags, Jessie, my assistant's, crash helmet – everything was his target. We soon learned not to disturb his domain! Cardy my white Cornish Rex was, I am told, a Champion Rex many times over and had been a stud cat. When I took him on I found (not unexpectedly given his history) that he was a manic sprayer whenever there were cats about. I tried to home him alone with an elderly lady but he howled for three weeks. 'I've worked with deprived and difficult children all my life,' she said, 'but none has been as troublesome as this cat.' Back he came and is now permanently ensconced in the bull pen I have converted into a room especially for him and his four white feline friends.

- The ideal cat for an indoor situation – either a flat, or a house on a main road – is a Persian, as they are more docile.
- If there's a stray cat in your area which is either a tomcat or a queen please either contact your local cat rescue centre or do a spot of cat rescue yourself. Recently we had a queen moggie living rough near our local stables. We homed her set of kittens and then borrowed a humane cat trap with tempting food inside from Sidlesham Cat Rescue. We caught her immediately, had her spayed and, as she was healthy and not causing any trouble, returned her to the stables where food was left out for her. She has more than paid for her keep by doing a daily spot of mousing.

WHAT'S OUT

- When getting a new cat do not let it out immediately – it should be kept in the house with a cat litter for two weeks. However you can buy a cat harness and lead if you want to introduce it to your garden before that.
- Do not be alarmed if your new cat does not eat for two or three days, it is quite a common phenomenon. If you get really anxious try titbits like fresh chicken, pilchards in tomato, a little liver or some live goats' or sheeps' yoghurt.
- If your new cat is sick upon arrival this is probably due to stress. If the sickness continues, starve the cat for twenty-four hours and then give it a diet of fresh chicken or rabbit and rice. If the cat has come from an unknown source the sickness may be due to negligence and lack of worming.
- Do not feed cats chocolate as it can be poisonous to them and be very wary about full-fat cheeses, yoghurts and milk. Many cats have a lactose intolerance and this can mean digestive upsets and bad skin conditions. Smoked meats and fish should be given very rarely because of the salt content, and carrots can sometimes cause trouble as cats cannot synthesise beta carotene.
- Food should not be left down as it will attract flies. However, it can be stored in the refrigerator and offered again. After twenty-four hours it should be thrown away.
- If you are introducing a new kitten to an old cat do not leave them unattended until you are convinced they are friends. A friend's old cat killed the new kitten when no one was looking.
- Don't judge too harshly a cat that sprays. Cats have few means of venting their disapproval and that unpleasant habit is one way they can show you their displeasure.
- Don't travel with a cat loose at any time. It can easily jump out of an open window, skylight or door, it can also cause accidents. There are many good cat carriers available. Personally I prefer the plastic ones, in case the cat pees with fright! When Blackie my black moggie urinated in his wicker basket on to the car seat on his second visit to the vet's, my husband said, 'If the last time you had been to the vet's you had had your nuts chopped off, you might have done the same!'
- Don't leave a kitten or young cat alone with the Christmas tree. The decorations make irresistible playthings and it may get hung or electrocuted by the fairy lights.

- Don't pinch your neighbour's cat. There are plenty of others at cat rescue centres who need homes. If you want to know whether the cat has an owner put a collar on it with a message attached. If you get a message back you will know the answer.

PREFERRED PRODUCTS

FELINE BEDS

My cats like all manner of beds. They tend to prefer the hooded variety in the winter, as the draughts are kept out on three sides, and absolutely adore the cats' cradles that you can hang on radiators. However, for all the expensive beds available, a cat can be just as happy with a sturdy cardboard box with Vet bed in the bottom or an old towel. Cats also have a mind of their own and will find their own comfortable places: your favourite armchair, on top of the airing cupboard in amongst the dirty (or clean) washing, and if you leave clothes lying around they may nest in them as they tend to love the scent of their owners. Sheba, my Siamese, who is particularly intelligent (she knows how to open door handles by swinging on them) will pull hot towels off the bathroom radiator and happily curl up in those.

FELINE ELECTRIC BLANKETS

I first acquired a mini-heat pad for Rexy, my arthritic Cornish Rex, when he had one leg run over by a car. The trouble was all the cats wanted to occupy it so now I have several. Much safer for kittens are the microwave oven pads which stay warm for some time and an old-fashioned hot water bottle is always a very welcome heater if your cat gets a chill. You can also find plastic beds with heating in the bottom which are hygienic, safe, practical and perfect for orphaned or sick kittens. An electric circuit breaker is a valuable asset when there are kittens or young cats around with a penchant for chewing electric wires.

CAT BOWLS

For the summer I prefer the large plastic bottles you can buy which fit upside down into a large dish so there is little chance of the cats drinking all the water. However, if they have access to the great outdoors they are just as likely to drink from a puddle. For food I prefer heavy-weight plastic bowls which are easily cleaned and cannot get broken. A cat timer bowl with a forty-eight hour clock can be a valuable asset if you keep irregular hours, as you can set it to open while you are out. However, Hodge, my Tonkinese, was always impatient and would throw it about the room, crash, bang, wallop, in an attempt to open it ahead of time!

CAT LITTERS

There are many varieties of cat litter and at different times I have tried almost all of them. Flaked wood shavings are the cheapest and biodegradable, however I do find the flakes tend to get spread about as they are lightweight. Biodegradable cat litters are the most ecological choices although they don't necessarily have the clumping action which makes cleaning easier. For kittens, how-ever, clumping products can be dangerous as they may get attached to and block the kittens' moist rear ends. Since they may also try to eat the litter a harmless wood or paper-based product is the best option. For older cats non-biodegradable products can be cheaper and more convenient, but ecologically they are not so good for our pressured planet.

CAT LITTER TRAYS

A simple cat litter tray is perfectly adequate for most cats, but if your cat particularly likes kicking the litter out of the tray or, as has happened with Baron, our young tabby, standing in the tray with his bottom over the edge, there are better alternatives. There are trays with hoods, some of which even have cat flap doors which stop the litter getting outside, and others have special rims which prevent the litter being spread about, although these don't resolve Baron's problem. If your cat is particularly hygienic you may require two trays. One girlfriend of mine even had to put a litter tray on top of her loo cistern as her Burmese had watched the humans in the bathroom and decided that was the place to go! Cats don't like dirty litter trays so in fairness to them you should clean them very frequently.

CAT FLEA PRODUCTS

An excellent anti-parasite shampoo with an anti-parasite tonic is Corpore Sano (available mail-order from the Sloane Square Health Shop in London). However, if you shampoo your cat be careful to do so on a hot day or dry it thoroughly so it doesn't get chilled.

Herbal flea collars

Herbal flea collars containing citronella, lemon grass, eucalyptus and lavender are non-chemical and excellent. However, the collars have to be kept topped up with the herbal remedies for maximum efficacity. Also check the cat's neck regularly for an allergic reaction.

Chemical flea collars

In the past the organo-phosphates in collars have been suspected of causing health problems in felines. Personally I hate putting chemicals anywhere near my cats, but the flea battle is such that sometimes one has to, as an unchecked flea infestation can cause anaemia, illness and even death. Three of my cats are all given chemical flea collars in the summer months as they are particularly prone to fleas. I remove the collars instantly if they seem under par and check their necks frequently for sores. A flea collar should not be put on a cat with scratches or sores around the neck and head area. If, like my Siamese, Sheba, your cat cannot wear a collar or have spot treatment then daily flea-combing is the answer, along with an occasional spray. At the moment Frontline is the spray I use rather sparingly. My friend Jennie, from Shirrin Persian Cat Rescue, prefers the chemical spot treatment on the back of the neck for her long-hairs and has used it most successfully.

Some products can be given orally, but I believe one should put only pure unadulterated foods into the digestive system. I will give brewers' yeast and garlic very happily as they are healthy, natural flea deterrents.

CAT FLAPS

In an attempt to resolve various cat fights I think I must have tried every cat flap available. The magnetic flap (either electric or battery) is a good idea as an escaping feline with the matching magnet around its neck can flee through its cat flap, leaving its pursuer perplexed the other side. However, it doesn't work when the escapee, feeling safe inside, goes back to the cat flap to torment its enemy. Its proximity to the cat flap releases the magnet and the pursuer can then enter and continue its pursuit!

Cat flaps without any locks are less than ideal because one day you may want to keep your cat in (maybe because of illness) or keep a marauding cat out. However, I have seen Toffee (my nervous Rex-Siamese) flee straight through a locked cat flap when we were trying to take her to the vet. Byron, the large British Short-Haired Tip, driven by a desire to beat up Rexy, the Cornish Rex, demolished two cat flaps before I finally installed a small, but more solid, dog flap with a secure lock, large screws and hinges!

CAT FOOD

I only feed commercially prepared foods in an emergency or when I have to go away.

Cans or Packs

Naturediet is 100 per cent accountable and uses very pure

ingredients. Hi-life uses a large proportion of fish in its cans. Hills Feline Growth, Feline Maintenance and IAMS are so full of good foods you will find you have to give less to a cat than a cheaper brand that is full of inferior feeds and moisture. Denes contains herbs and seaweed.

All-in-one Biscuit Meals

There are many on the market but the only ones I will buy, as they have either less or no additives, chemicals, preservatives, colourants or sugars are: James Wellbeloved, Burns, Denes, Nutro, Hills Science Diet, Eukanuba IAMS, Techni-cal and Arden Grange.

DIETS FOR
DIFFERENT AGES

In the wild kittens and cats would all have eaten the same freshly killed prey of mice, voles, small birds and rabbits. The stomachs of their victims would have been full of grasses, grains, vegetables and fruit, and felines fed on such a natural diet would have had few problems in old age. Unfortunately in our modern world of pollutants, pesticides and chemicals that isn't the case and the requirements of kittens, adult cats and geriatrics in a domestic situation are very different. Kittens must eat the right things for optimum development and it is not advisable to give them cheap all-in-one dried foods or semi-moist preparations. Equally, a feline old age pensioner may not be able to cope with the impure foods it withstood in its adolescence and adulthood. If a cat's nutrition is not at the optimum level its health is bound to suffer in later years. Its immune system will be low and it will be vulnerable to all manner of diseases unless the symptoms are spotted early and the diet radically altered.

Kittens should be naturally weaned as mother's milk is best and keeping motherless kittens healthy from a young age poses a real problem. They need to be kept clean and warm and to be fed little and often. Feeding kittens of three weeks was, I found, quite a challenge: tiny amounts of goats' milk and goats' yoghurt, oat milk and bottled water were the main drinks, but the most beneficial food was minced free range chicken breast mixed with a little water in a child's blender, with a few drops of feline liquid vitamins. I also occasionally gave them a little organic porridge mixed with a small amount of live goats' yoghurt. Live yoghurt contains stomach enzymes which can help the digestive system but at the same time one has to watch out for a lactose intolerance to dairy products. At three weeks they needed to be fed four times a day.

First meal:	Finely minced chicken breast with water and liquid vitamins.
Second meal:	Organic porridge with a little live goats' yoghurt.
Third meal:	Finely minced chicken breast with a little water and liquid vitamins.
Fourth meal:	Organic scrambled eggs – just the eggs, no milk, butter or oil – with a little spirulina or premium grade chlorella powder added.

At five weeks most kittens have a large percentage of their baby teeth and if necessary can slowly transfer to commercial food. Of the cans I prefer Denes chicken and rabbit kitten food, and of the dried complete meals James Wellbeloved's and Nutro's kitten feeds. But if you have to feed just dried food do make sure the kittens are drinking enough pure water so as not to get dehydrated.

From twelve weeks until six months the kittens should have at least three meals a day. I have been feeding my kittens:

1. Local rabbit or pheasant with a feline mineral powder.
2. Organic porridge with a little live goats' yoghurt.
3. Organic chicken and rice with powdered feline multi vitamins and minerals.

Six months onwards I feed my cats two meals a day:

1. Chicken/turkey and rice with a feline mineral powder.
2. Rabbit/pheasant and millet with a feline multi-vitamin and mineral.

For the geriatric cats I will add a little vitamin C powder to the food as well. Twice a week I will also give cooked cod or coley (cod for more sensitive tummies) and twice a week I mix a little chicken liver in with the meat meals. If I have to go away the cats are given Naturediet, Denes and Hi-life cans and the Chinchilla-Rex, Camilla, is fed tiny Gourmet cans containing 4 per cent chicken and 4 per cent liver, simply because she refuses to eat any other canned food. As a mid-day treat they often get a small amount of James Wellbeloved, Burns, Nutro, Hills, Iams Alden Grange or Techni-cal biscuit.

Needless to say my cats' coats are all very glossy and that includes the geriatrics and all, except Camilla and Byron (whom I rescued aged ten), have their teeth.

If fed well, the proper amount and allowed a certain amount of exercise along with an unlimited amount of love and affection, a feline should stay lithe and healthy into its senior citizenship. It should end up a very contented, purring old age pensioner cat.

RECIPES FOR CATS WITH SPECIFIC DISEASES

All the following recipes should have taurine and feline vitamin and mineral supplements and extra vitamin C added either in or after food:

LIVER DISEASE

After a fast of twenty-four hours a perfect recipe would be:

1 cup roasted breast of organic chicken diced with a tablespoon of bottled water.

$\frac{1}{2}$ cup cooked oats.

$\frac{1}{2}$ cup cooked broccoli and a teaspoon of raw grated beetroot and parsley.

Mix all ingredients together and serve at room temperature.

This should be sufficient for at least four meals for an average size cat.

CANCER

1 cup raw rabbit if you can obtain it from a good, wild source. If the source is doubtful either roast or boil it.

$\frac{1}{2}$ cup of cooked millet or polenta.

$\frac{1}{2}$ cup finely diced cabbage boiled with organic garlic.

Mix together and serve at room temperature.

Do not give parsley, parsnips or celery as these are said to be carcinogenic. This should be enough for at least four servings for an average size cat.

KIDNEY DISEASE

1 cup roasted turkey breast minced with a tablespoon of bottled water.

$\frac{1}{2}$ cup boiled white rice and one diced cooked garlic clove.

$\frac{1}{2}$ cup cooked broccoli with grated raw beetroot.

Mix well and serve at room temperature.

This should be sufficient for at least four meals for an average size cat.

DIABETES

1 cup raw rabbit (cooked if not from a reliable source)

$\frac{1}{2}$ cup using equal measures of cooked brown rice and diced cooked beans and peas.

Combine ingredients and serve at room temperature.

This should be enough for at least four meals for an average size cat.

FIP, FIV and FeLV

1 cup chicken breast stuffed with fine slivers of garlic and rosemary then roasted.
$\frac{1}{2}$ cup white rice boiled with one chicken liver.
$\frac{1}{2}$ cup cooked broccoli with one tablespoon cooked beetroot.

Mix all ingredients together and serve at room temperature.
This should be sufficient for at least four meals for an average size cat.

(Daily feline vitamin and mineral supplements will be necessary for the remainder of the cat's life to boost its immune system and keep the disease at bay.)

To make cooked rice more palatable I often stuff the inside of a chicken or turkey with rice and garlic slivers and then enfold the bird in a clay brick or silver foil in a roasting pan. I cook it for an hour and a half on a high temperature. The advantage of cooking this way is that the meat stays moist and does not dry out and the rice absorbs the flavour of the chicken or turkey. The fat at the bottom of the brick or pan should, however, be thrown away.

COMMERCIAL
CAT FOOD

I used to go into supermarkets and come out with a trolley laden with canned dog and cat food, but no longer. Since writing *Canine Care and Cuisine* and *Cat Care and Cuisine* I have started to look at the small print on the back of the cans. Before I did so I thought 'WITH CHICKEN' meant precisely that; I didn't realise that in many cases it meant a paltry 4 per cent. The rest goes under the bland description 'animal or vegetable derivatives' together with moisture, caramels (sugars), colourants, additives and preservatives. Could somebody please tell me what an animal or vegetable derivative is?!

I am as guilty as the next person of wanting to lead an 'instant' life when it comes to the preparation of food for both myself and my animals. However, I do believe I have a right to know exactly what I am feeding my pets. If I am not allowed to know I would rather buy meat, poultry, fish, fresh vegetables, pulses and grains, cook in bulk and add the necessary feline vitamin and mineral supplements to keep my cats in optimum health.

In the *Earth Island Journal* (Fall 1990 and Summer 1996), which is published in the USA, they ran articles explaining how euthanased dogs and cats were sent to the pet food rendering plants. There, incredibly, they were boiled up with the other miscellanea from the meat industry and put into pet foods. I am not suggesting that this has happened in the UK, but I would still like to know precisely what 'derivatives' are. In England manufacturers stopped using offal, which included potentially infectious BSE material, in April 1989. This was not a moment too soon, as there have been seventy-one reported incidences of the fatal BSE-related disease, called feline spongiform encephalopathy, in cats since 1990.

Unfortunately there are very few makes of pet food that I like. Streets ahead is Naturediet as it is very pure and all the ingredients are accounted for (cats will even eat their dog food, which is most unusual) and after this comes Hi-Life, which has a high fish content in its cans, and I sometimes give my cats Denes because of the herbal and seaweed contents.

There are good brands of all-in-one dried foods, but personally I would not want to give my cats just cereal nuggets. I worry that they may dehydrate if they don't drink enough water with the biscuit. James Wellbeloved, John Burns and Nutro Kitten food are my favourites, as they seem to be additive, colourant and preservative free and include substantial vitamin supplements. I also give Hills Science Diet, Arden Grange, Eukanuba and Techni-cal. They do tend to be the more expensive brands, but I am afraid that you do get what you pay for.

The sick kittens and cats I have restored to health have never been able to tolerate the cheaper brands – they gave them diarrhoea – whilst others have been cured on a diet of James Wellbeloved, Burns, Nutro or Hills. My young cats Duke and Baron have done very well on Nutro, Sheba my Siamese was cured of tummy problems on Hills and little Alfie who has been allergic to everything except rabbit, pheasant and turkey, enjoys James Wellbeloved turkey and rice dog biscuit – but only as a treat, as the protein ratio is wrong for cats.

As for some of the semi-moist packets of cat food, the amount of additives, preservatives and sugars, not to mention that word 'derivatives' again, makes them unacceptable to my rescued and often sickly cats.

MEATY MEALS

'Honest as the cat when the meat is out of reach.'

Proverb

Cats are very definitely carnivores, requiring larger amounts of protein than dogs along with a supply of the amino acid taurine which is found in meat. A cat may develop heart problems or die within a year if taurine is removed from its diet. In the wild cats would devour mice, voles, small rodents, small rabbits and small birds (though my first cat Kim did, unfortunately, tackle pheasants and ducks!). Veterinary opinions are divided as to which meats to feed cats, but when I feed mine I prefer to keep as close to nature as possible, serving up predominantly rabbit, chicken, pheasant, turkey and, very occasionally, lamb, hardly ever beef (some cats are allergic to beef) and never pork (there may be a risk of trichinosis). With so many cats I often have to prepare different menus as they all have their pet hates: Coley, my black and white moggie, liked beef and hated fish, Hodge, my Tonkinese, disliked beef and loved fish and Alfie my orphaned seven-month-old kitten is allergic to chicken though fine with rabbit! It would be nice to be able to feed raw meat, but as cats are susceptible to parasites and salmonella, on the whole it is ill-advised these days. Equally, over-cooking destroys the vitamin content, which should be replaced with a good feline vitamin and mineral supplement. A small percentage of cooked grains and vegetables is also beneficial to a cat's health. If you are having difficulty introducing new items to an older cat's diet the vegetables can be diced finely with the grains and mixed into their normal diet, and you can increase the amounts as their palates become better adjusted.

Given the amounts of antibiotics, steroids and chemicals used on animals today, not to mention the fear of BSE in beef and scrapie in sheep, we recommend organic foods. At the back of the book we have included the address of the 'Soil Association Directory of Organic Farm Shops and Box Schemes'.

Juiette de Bairacli Levy, the herbalist, recommends uncooked meaty bones at the end of a meal as cooked bones can splinter. However, these days they would have to come from a fresh, organic source so that no parasites or unpleasant diseases were transmitted. They certainly are nature's way of cleaning teeth, particularly after sugary, processed foods.

BACK TO BASICS

'If cats were human, they'd watch *Masterpiece Theater*, drive a German import car, belong to a country club, melt Brie before serving, subscribe to *The New York Times Book Review* every Sunday, and think Harley-Davidson was a law firm.

Dogs on the other hand, would watch *Roseanne*, belong to the Price Club, have a plastic liner in their pocket for their leaky pen, and consider Pavarotti an Italian entrée.'

Quotable Cats
by Emma Bombeck

The following recipes are basic stand-bys which can be made in advance and stored in airtight containers in the refrigerator. You can add Crunchy Crumbs or Kat Kibble to increase the bulk or Fish Brew, Meaty Brew or Veggie Brew to moisten your cat's main meal.

CRUNCHY CRUMBS

Rub any amount of wholemeal bread into breadcrumbs. Spread the breadcrumbs on a baking tray and sprinkle on some crushed, cooked garlic and cook in the oven at 300°F for 30 minutes.

KAT KIBBLE

4 oz (115g/1 cup) Shipton Mill 5 Cereal Blend – malted wheat flakes, barley flakes, sunflower seeds, millet and oats
2 oz (55g/$\frac{1}{2}$ cup) Shipton Mill organic 100% wholemeal flour
$\frac{1}{4}$ teaspoon Marmite (Yeast Extract, Vegemite or Vitamite)
2 tablespoons filtered water
2 teaspoons sesame oil

Mix the 5 Cereal Blend and the wholemeal flour together. Boil the water and add the Marmite. Pour the Marmite mixture and the sesame oil on the dry ingredients and mix well. Spread on a greased baking tray and cook in the oven at 300°F for 30 minutes.

FISH BREW

1 lb (455g) fish (heads, tails, skin and bones)
30 fl oz (1½ pints UK/1¾ pints approx. USA) filtered water
1 floret of broccoli, chopped
1 onion, chopped
1 stick of celery, chopped
a pinch of herbes de Provence

Put all the ingredients in a saucepan. Cover and bring to the boil.
Simmer for 45 minutes – any longer and it will start to taste bitter.
Strain the brew through a fine sieve.

MEATY BREW

1 lb (455g) any combination of beef/lamb/chicken and rabbit
(meat, bones, gristle)
40 fl oz (2 pints UK/2½ pints USA) cold filtered water
1 teaspoon Bovril or Marmite (Yeast Extract, Vegemite or Vitamite)
½ teaspoon wheatgerm oil
1 beetroot, sliced
½ onion, sliced
1 turnip, sliced

Put the meat, water, Bovril/Marmite and wheatgerm oil in a
saucepan. Cover and bring to the boil. Simmer for 1 hour or
longer if you want to have more gelatine and calcium drawn out
of the bones and meat. Add the vegetables. Bring to the boil and
simmer for a further 30 minutes. Strain. If the meat was fatty, skim
off the excess fat when it has cooled.

VEGGIE BREW

3 oz (85g/1 cup) leek, sliced
2 oz (55g/½ cup) celery, chopped
4 oz (115g/just under 1 cup) swede, peeled and chopped
3 oz (85g/½ heaped cup) sweet potato, cubed
1 oz (30g/¼ cup) cabbage, sliced
1 teaspoon Marmite (Yeast Extract, Vegemite or Vitamite)
30 fl oz (1½ pints UK/1¾ pints approx. USA) filtered water

Put all the ingredients in a saucepan. Cover and bring to the boil.
Simmer for 35 minutes. Strain off the liquid.

REYNOLDS' RABBIT RELISH

'Cat! who hast passed thy grand climacteric,
How many mice and rats hast in thy days
Destroyed? How many tit bits stolen? Gaze
With those bright languid segments green, and prick
Those velvet ears - but prithee do not stick
Thy latent talons in me, and up-raise
Thy gentle mew, and tell me all thy frays
Of fish and mice, and rats and tender chick.'

'To Mrs Reynolds' Cat', *The Complete Poems*
by John Keats

9 oz (255g) fresh rabbit loin cutlets
2 oz (55g/$\frac{2}{3}$ cup) cauliflower florets, chopped
$\frac{1}{4}$ teaspoon garlic, crushed
10 fl oz (285ml/1$\frac{1}{4}$ cups) tomato juice
1$\frac{3}{4}$ oz (50g/$\frac{1}{4}$ cup) brown rice

Put all the ingredients in a casserole dish. Bake in the oven uncovered at 350°F for 1$\frac{1}{2}$ hours. Allow to cool. Remove rabbit flesh from the bones and cut into small pieces.

Yields: approx. 1 lb 2 oz/510g

PERSIAN PHEASANT PILAFF

Florence Nightingale owned more than sixty Persian cats in her lifetime and many of them were named after distinguished 19th-century men; for example, Bismarck, Disraeli and Gladstone. Her cats are reputed to have travelled with her wherever she went and by observing them she learnt many lessons about life; though one thing she never did discover was where the stains came from that mysteriously appeared on her paperwork...

6 oz (170g) fresh pheasant breast fillets
$\frac{1}{4}$ clove garlic, crushed
filtered water
2 tablespoons sweetcorn, cooked
1 oz (30g/$\frac{1}{4}$ cup) cooked brown rice

Place the pheasant and garlic in a casserole dish. Cover with filtered water. Bake in the oven at 325°F for 1$\frac{1}{2}$ hours. Chop up the pheasant and mix with the sweetcorn and brown rice. Moisten the meal with some of the stock.

Yields: approx. 8 oz/230g

LUCHTIGERN LIVER

The old Irish name for a cat, Luchtigern, translates into 'Lord of the Mice'.

4 oz (115g/½ cup) chicken livers, chopped
1½ oz (45g/¼ cup) lamb, chopped
¼ teaspoon tarragon, chopped
1½ oz (45g/¾ cup) olive bread, crumbled
1 free range egg, beaten
5 fl oz (140ml/¾ cup) Meaty Brew (page 84)
1 tablespoon brussels sprouts, cooked and mashed

Mix all the ingredients together, except the brussels sprouts, and place in a small loaf tin. Bake in the oven at 360°F for 1 hour. Serve with the brussels sprouts.

Yields: 11½ oz/325g

BONA BALLS

8 oz (230g/1⅓ cups) turkey mince
1 oz (30g/½ cup) organic brown bread, crumbled
1 teaspoon Parmesan cheese, grated
1 teaspoon parsley, chopped
1 free range egg, beaten
1 oz (30g/¼ cup) Scottish porridge oats with bran
1 oz (30g/¼ cup) organic wholemeal flour
1 (400g) tin chopped Italian tomatoes with olive oil and garlic
2 fl oz (55ml/¼ cup) Meaty Brew (page 84)
1 bay leaf

Mix together thoroughly the turkey mince, bread, Parmesan cheese, parsley, egg and oats. Form into small round balls and roll in the flour. Gently heat the tomatoes, Meaty Brew and bay leaf in a deep frying pan. Add the meat balls. Bring to the boil, cover and simmer for 45 minutes. Remove the bay leaf.

Yields: approx. 18 meat balls

MEATY MEAL

In *The Cat's Paradise* by Émile Zola, we are introduced to a two-year-old cat that was 'the fattest and most naive cat in existence'. He had all the attention, luxury and comforts any cat could wish for and his 'food was equally excellent; never just bread, or soup, but always meat, carefully chosen meat'. But he was bored. All he ever dreamed of was being able to escape onto the tiles and romp and have fun with the other cats he'd seen from afar.

One day the kitchen window was left open and he made a dash for his freedom. He was soon befriended by three cats, one of whom – a tomcat – offered to teach him how to survive street-life. He 'drank from the gutters, and never did sugared milk taste half as fine!' But scavenging in the garbage for food, getting cold and soaking wet from the rain soon palled and he wanted to go home. So the tomcat took him home. He was severely punished by his mistress, but afterwards as he lay in front of the warm fire having just devoured a delicious meaty meal ...

3 oz (85g/½ cup) lamb mince, boiled
3 oz (85g/½ cup) chicken mince, boiled
a pinch of mint, chopped
½ oz (15g/⅛ cup) courgette (zucchini), cooked and mashed
½ oz (15g/⅛ cup) peas, cooked and mashed
2 tablespoons cooked couscous

Mix all the ingredients together.

Yields: approx. 5¾ oz/160g

MADAME HELVETIUS' POUSSIN POTAGE

Madame Helvetius, a Parisian courtesan whom Benjamin Franklin had aspirations to marrying, had eighteen cats who were partial to the delicacy of chicken breasts.

1 poussin (approx. 14 oz/400g)
extra virgin olive oil
a pinch of garlic granules
1½ oz (45g/⅓ cup) cooked bulghur
1 tablespoon sweetcorn, cooked and puréed
1 tablespoon peas, cooked and puréed
6 fl oz (170g/just over ¾ cup) Meaty Brew (page 84)

Place the poussin on a roasting rack. Brush with a little extra virgin olive oil and sprinkle on the garlic granules. Bake in the oven for 1½ hours at 375°F. Allow to cool before removing all the bones and finely cutting up the flesh. Mix with the bulghur, sweetcorn and peas. Add the Meaty Brew to produce a thick soup consistency.

Yields: 14½ oz/415g

CLEO PATRA STEW

Mike Tomkies, the wildlife photographer and writer, tells his extraordinary experiences with wildcats in Scotland in *My Wilderness Wildcats*. Here we have an insight into the eating habits of the wildcats – Cleo, Patra, Freddy, Mia and Sylvesturr:

'... we had just returned from a long high trek, when we found Patra in the workshop raiding the box of dog sausages. Fat and heavy, her tail really bushy now, she spat and shot out as we entered. And at dusk both kits came to feed with Cleo on the rock.

Next evening after feeding, I made myself a stew into which I poured some old oats without checking them first. It tasted awful so I tipped it onto the grass outside and kept watch, as I made a fresh stew, thinking Patra would scent it. To my surprise, Cleo arrived, closely followed by Freddy and Mia. They ate a little but weren't hungry, then took off again for the west wood, Cleo leading.

...

After returning in the boat, I went down to the feed rock. Nearly all the meat and milk had now gone, and I startled Freddy who had been calmly scraping moss and leaves over both bowls, standing high on three legs while scraping away with his right front paw. This real wildcat trait was a perfect example of inherited instinct from Sylvesturr, who was now scraping even larger mounds of debris over his nightly left-overs against the slugs and the new onslaught of the sexton beetles.'

4 oz (115g/1 cup) rabbit, chopped
4 oz (115g/1 cup) lamb, chopped
a pinch of rosemary, chopped
1 oz (30g/⅓ heaped cup) cauliflower florets, chopped
1 teaspoon Marmite (Yeast Extract, Vegemite or Vitamite)

$\frac{1}{2}$ oz (15g/just under $\frac{1}{4}$ cup) Scottish porridge oats with bran
20 fl oz (570ml/2$\frac{1}{2}$ cups) filtered water
1$\frac{1}{2}$ oz (45g/$\frac{1}{3}$ cup) cooked brown rice

Put all the ingredients in a covered saucepan. Bring to the boil and simmer for 1$\frac{3}{4}$ hours.

Yields: approx. 11$\frac{1}{2}$ oz/330g

CROOKED KITTY CASSEROLE

'There was a crooked man, and he went a crooked mile,
He found a crooked sixpence against a crooked stile:
He bought a crooked cat, which caught a crooked mouse,
And they all lived together in a little crooked house.'

Traditional Nursery Rhyme

1 jar baby food – Vegetable and Chicken Casserole (without carrots or dairy products)
$\frac{1}{8}$ teaspoon Marmite
1 raw free range egg yolk, beaten
1 drop liquid vitamins for children
1 heaped tablespoon Crunchy Crumbs (page 83)

Gently heat the Vegetable and Chicken Casserole according to the instructions on the jar. Add the Marmite and stir until it is well blended. Remove from the heat. Add the egg yolk and liquid vitamins. Sprinkle the Crunchy Crumbs on top.

Yields: approx. 6 oz/170g

FOOD FOR THOUGHT

I

'A cat in distress,
Nothing more, nor less;
Good folks, I must faithfully tell ye,
As I am a sinner,
It waits for some dinner,
To stuff out its own little belly.

V

But this poor little cat
Only wanted a rat,
To stuff out its own little maw;
And it were as good
Some people had such food,
To make them hold their jaw!'

'Verses on a Cat', *Shelley Poetical Works*
edited by Thomas Hutchinson

3 oz (85g/just under ½ cup) turkey mince
a cooked garlic clove
¼ teaspoon Marmite (Yeast Extract, Vegemite or Vitamite)
12 fl oz (340ml/1½ cups) filtered water
3 oz (85g/⅔ cup) fine beans, trimmed and finely chopped
1 tablespoon tomato juice

Place the turkey mince, garlic, Marmite and filtered water in a saucepan. Bring to the boil and simmer for 5 minutes. Add the beans and simmer for a further 5 minutes. Drain. Add the tomato juice.

Yields: 6 oz/170g

FISH FODDER

'There is a propensity belonging to common house-cats that is very remarkable; I mean their violent fondness for fish, which appears to be their most favourite food...'

The Natural History of Selborne
by Gilbert White

pollyanna pickering

Fish is not a cat's natural food, although I suppose Turkish Vans, the swimming cats, might disagree with me. I tend to give fish once or twice a week as they are a good source of protein, magnesium, iron and selenium, but no more than that and certainly not tuna. It is ironic that most cats are tuna junkies when it is the fish that most disagrees with them. It can cause skin problems, depleting vitamin E in the body, and can upset the pancreas, stomach, liver and kidneys, and even cause urinary infections. I have given my cats tuna as a treat but always with the addition of two drops of vitamin E oil on the food. Coley is the cheapest of fish but it is fatty and has caused stomach upsets in some of the kittens I have reared, whereas cod is much more easily digested. Mackerel, herring and sardines have the highest levels of fatty acids which maintain a shiny coat, and pilchards or mackerel in tomato sauce are often used to tempt a cat that has been off its food. Cats can choke on fish bones and fish heads just like humans, so you must be meticulous about removing every bone before serving. Haddock, sole, hake and skate are also good fish to cook, but raw fish must be avoided as it contains the enzyme thiaminase which destroys vitamin B1. However, after cooking fish can be kept in a refrigerator for up to twenty-four hours before re-serving it cold. Fish should never be re-heated, and can be kept only for a day and a night in a refrigerator. A fish meal lacks calcium and vitamin A and should only be a small part of a varied diet including meat, vegetables, pulses and cereals. Cod liver oil can be beneficial but only in very small amounts. Be careful not to overdose with vitamins A and D if they are already included in a multivitamin formula you may be giving.

TROUT TREAT

The following quote comes from *Magnus The Orkney Cat* by Kathleen Russell and Marion Campbell:

'Mr Blenkinsop had a grand day at the fishing. Magnus helped to prepare the trout. And got his share as a reward.'

2 oz (55g/½ cup) trout fillet, cooked and mashed
1 oz (30g/¼ cup) cooked American Easy Cook and Wild Rice
1 mangetout, cooked and chopped
¼ teaspoon brewers' yeast

Mix all the ingredients together.

Yields: approx. 4 oz/115g

FISH PAWS

'All cats love fish but fear to wet their paws.'

Proverb

1 cod fillet (approx. 5¾ oz/160g)
a pinch of dill, chopped
1 bay leaf
8 fl oz (230ml/1 cup) water
4 fl oz (115ml/½ cup) goats' milk
1 oz (30g/½ cup) broccoli, cooked & puréed
2 heaped tablespoons cooked brown rice
½ teaspoon brewers' yeast

Put the fish, dill and bay leaf in a saucepan and pour over the water and goats' milk. Bring to the boil and simmer for 7-8 minutes. Drain, discarding the bay leaf. Flake the fish, removing any bones. Mix with the broccoli, brown rice and brewers' yeast.

Yields: approx. 7 oz/200g

PUSS IN BOOTS' BREAM

'When the cat had got what he'd asked for, he looked the picture of elegance with his new boots. Slinging the bag round his neck and using his front paws to pull the draw-strings, he padded off to a warren where there were a great number of rabbits. Putting some bran, endive and chicory into his bag and lying down at full length as though he were dead, he waited for some young rabbit, unused to the tricks of this world, to stick its head into the bag to eat what he'd put into it.'

'Puss In Boots' by Charles Perrault
The Faber Book of Favourite Fairy Tales

1 sea bream – head removed (approx. 11 oz/315g)
1 sachet Bouquet Garni
2 teaspoons live goats' yoghurt
1 oz (30g/¼ cup) courgette (zucchini), cooked and mashed
1 heaped tablespoon cooked millet

Put the Bouquet Garni sachet in the middle of the sea bream. Wrap the fish in foil and bake in the oven at 375°F for 30 minutes. Remove the sachet. Flake the fish, de-bone and discard the skin. Add the goats' yoghurt. Mix in the fish with the courgette and millet.

Yields: 8¾ oz/250g

INDEPENDENCE DAY DISH/POO JONES' POACHED SALMON

Poo Jones was the beloved Siamese cat belonging to the legendary actress Vivien Leigh. Poo Jones and Vivien travelled to England across the Atlantic on the *Queen Elizabeth* in 1960, during which time they had a daily ritual of promenading around the deck together. After enduring six months' quarantine, one can imagine poached salmon would indeed have been a welcome treat for Poo Jones.

'At night, as moonlight fell on the waters, there'd be paper-and-pencil games by the firelight indoors, where Poo Jones, liberated from quarantine, occupied the hearthrug.'

Vivien – The Life of Vivien Leigh
by Alexander Walker

1 (6¾ oz/190g) fresh salmon steak
1 bay leaf
1 dwarf corn, cooked and chopped
2 mangetout, cooked and chopped
1 tablespoon live goats' yoghurt
1 oz (30g/¼ cup) cooked American Easy Cook and Wild Rice

Place the salmon and the bay leaf in a saucepan. Cover with cold water. Bring to the boil and simmer for 5 minutes. Turn off the heat and let the salmon rest in the hot water for 10 minutes. Drain the water and discard the bay leaf. Remove any bones from the salmon. Mix together the salmon, corn, mangetout, goats' yoghurt and rice.

Yields: approx. 6 oz/170g

At any age, after six months' imprisonment, a pet welcomes the comforts of home and most of all home-cooked meals.

HOLLY GOLIGHTLY HALLOWE'EN HOKI

Orangey was the name of the cat who played the part of Cat in the 1961 film *Breakfast at Tiffany's*. Cat belonged to Holly Golightly, the character portrayed so memorably by Audrey Hepburn.

3 oz (85g) New Zealand hoki fillet
16 fl oz (455ml/2 cups) filtered water
a pinch of herbes de Provence
1 tablespoon beetroot, grated
$\frac{1}{2}$ teaspoon pumpkin seeds, ground
1 heaped tablespoon cooked polenta

Poach the hoki fillet in the filtered water with the herbes de Provence for 10–12 minutes. Drain the fish. Flake and remove any bones. Mix with the beetroot, pumpkin seeds and polenta.

Yields: approx. $4\frac{1}{4}$ oz/125g

WHITING FOR A WHITE CAT

In 'The White Cat', featured in W. W. Jacobs' collection of short stories entitled *Captain's All*, we come across a traveller drinking a mug of ale at the *Cauliflower* taproom. He is stroking a cat while listening to an old man telling him about 'a white cat, with one yaller eye and one blue one' that belonged to a man called Clark, Joe Clark's uncle. Apparently Joe Clark couldn't stand the cat but knowing he was a beneficiary of his uncle's will made out he liked the cat and he would 'take it little drops o' cream and tid-bits o' meat', and old Clark was so pleased that 'e promised 'im that he should 'ave the cat along with all the other property when 'e was dead.

Young Joe said he couldn't thank 'im enough, and the old man, who 'ad been ailing a long time, made 'im come up every day to teach 'im 'ow to take care of it arter he was gone. He taught Joe 'ow to cook its meat and then chop it up fine: 'ow it liked a clean saucer every time for its milk; and 'ow he wasn't to make a noise when it was asleep.'

1 whiting fillet (approx. 5 oz/140g)
8 fl oz (230ml/1 cup) goats' milk
a sprinkling of chives, chopped
½ oz (15g/⅛ cup) organic cornflour
1 tablespoon cavolo nero (black cabbage), cooked and puréed
1½ oz (45g/⅓ cup) cooked brown rice

Put the whiting, goats' milk and chives in a shallow casserole dish. Bake in the oven at 360°F for 20 minutes. Drain, retaining the liquid. Flake the fish, removing any bones. Mix the whiting with the black cabbage and brown rice. Moisten with the stock.

Yields: approx. 8 oz/230g

PURRFECT PLAICE

Three little kittens they lost their mittens,
And they began to cry,
Oh! mother dear,
We greatly fear
Our mittens we have lost.

What! lost your mittens, you bad little kittens,
Then you shall have no pie.
Mee-ow, mee-ow, mee-ow.
Then you shall have no pie.

Three little kittens they found their mittens,
And they began to cry,
Oh! mother dear,
See here, see here,
Our mittens we have found.

What! found your mittens, you good little kittens,
Then you shall have some pie.
Purr, purr, purrs.
Yes, you shall have some pie.

Traditional Nursery Rhyme

$\frac{1}{2}$ plaice, filleted (approx. 3 oz/85g)
1 free range egg, beaten
a pinch of thyme, chopped
1 heaped tablespoon cooked brown rice
1 heaped teaspoon kale, cooked and chopped

Coat the fish with some of the egg. Place the plaice on a greased baking tray and sprinkle on the thyme. Put under a moderate to high grill for 5 minutes. Turn and pour a little more of the egg over the fish. Grill for a further 3 minutes. Cut up the fish, removing any bones. Mix with the brown rice and kale.

Yields: approx. 4 oz/115g

RUNCIBLE RED SNAPPER

'And all the sailors and the Admirals cried,
When they saw him nearing the further side, –
"He has gone to fish, for his Aunt Jobiska's
Runcible Cat with crimson whiskers."'

'The Pobble Who Has No Toes', *Laughable Lyrics*
by Edward Lear

5 oz (140g/1 cup) red snapper, grilled, de-boned and flaked
1 heaped tablespoon cooked millet
1 heaped tablespoon pumpkin, cooked and puréed

Mix all the ingredients together.

Yields: approx. 6 oz/170g

MINI'S MOUTHFUL

Cats are often mentioned in wills and large sums of money are left along with instructions of how and by whom they are to be cared for. To give you an example, here is an extract from Miss Topping's will which was printed in *The Times* in 1843. (She died in Vendôme in May 1841.)

'I desire that there shall be raised from the most easily convertible part of my property a capital sum sufficient to produce 800 francs a year, which shall be paid quarterly to such person as I may name ... on condition of taking the care and nourishment of my three favourite cats, Nina, Fan-fan and Mini... The person [so] appointed shall live on a groundfloor, to which shall adjoin a terrace easy of access and a garden enclosed within walls, of which they shall have full and free enjoyment... They are to sleep in the house, and therefore are to be shut up after their supper.'

1 free range boiled egg, peeled and mashed
1 tin (120g) sardines in tomato sauce, drained
1 tablespoon spinach, cooked and chopped
2 teaspoons live goats' yoghurt
1 tablespoon cooked brown rice
$\frac{1}{4}$ teaspoon brewers' yeast

Mix all the ingredients together.

Yields: approx. 6 oz/170g

DECEPTIVE DIET

'A widow kept a favourite cat.
At first a gentle creature;
But when he was grown sleek and fat,
With many a mouse, and many a rat,
He soon disclosed his nature.'

A Fable of the Widow and Her Cat
by Jonathan Swift

2½ oz (70g/½ cup) hake, poached and flaked
2½ oz (70g/½ cup) haddock, poached and flaked
1 oz (30g/½ cup) organic brown bread, crumbled
½ teaspoon brussels sprouts, cooked

Combine all the ingredients. Put them in a blender and mix until smooth.

Yields: approx. 6 oz/170g

VEGETARIAN OR VEGAN VICTUALS

'Cats know how to obtain food without labour, shelter without confinement and love without penalties.'

W. L. George

It is possible for a cat to be a vegetarian or vegan provided that the owner knows what he or she is doing with protein and carbohydrate ratios and the addition of taurine and the correct feline vitamins and minerals. Many cats are allergic to dairy products and have a lactose intolerance which can cause diarrhoea and bad skin conditions. Eggs too are not without their problems, as raw egg white destroys the B vitamin biotin, and because of the danger of salmonella eggs must be cooked. If possible the eggs should be organic and free range as battery eggs contain little lecithin or methionine.

By far the safest option if you wish your cat to be vegan is to obtain a Vegecat or Vegekit pack from the Vegan Society. The formulation takes into account the calorific density and the nutritional needs of cats and kittens generally and is highly recommended by the eminent veterinarian David H. Jaggar MRCVS BVM & S. Kittens can be given Vegekit at about three to four weeks of age and can be weaned at about eight to ten weeks. They should go on to Vegecat when they are twelve months old.

The Vegan Society products have been in use since 1986, and apart from providing thousands of cats with all the nutrients they need for a healthy, balanced diet they do reduce the numbers of other animals killed specifically for the pet food industry.

According to the Vegan Society some favourite foods may be: spirulina (algae) powder (which my cats Duchess, Duke, Baron, Alfie, Abbie and Cardy adore) olive oil, avocado, tomato sauce, Tartex and yeast extract and possibly melon, cucumber, cooked brussels sprouts, broccoli and sugar-free baked beans. I have found that sick kittens do well with organic porridge as one of their meals and corn, maize and millet are also popular. I often try to stop my cats stealing the hens' grain in the barn, but as it is organic it doesn't do any harm. Some felines can have a wheat allergy but organic spelt wheat (obtainable from Shipton Mill) may be more tolerated.

If you are not buying the Vegecat product, when feeding a cat vegetarian food Dr Richard Pitcairn, the American vet, recommends the addition of fifty or more milligrams of taurine and up to two teaspoons of plain protein powder from egg albumen per day. To make sure your cat is obtaining maximum nourishment do vary the recipes. Recently I read of a cat that was predominantly vegetarian living to the age of thirty-two, so it can be a healthy meat-free alternative if done correctly with sufficient taurine, protein, calcium and feline vitamins and minerals.

Protein ratings (out of 100g): Eggs 94; Milk 82 (pasteurised 70); UHT 20; Cheese 70–75; Brown rice 70; Buckwheat 65; Broccoli and brussels sprouts 60; Soy beans 61; Lentils 30; Corn 72; Cauliflower 60; Potato 60; Oats 65; Pumpkin seeds 60; Sesame seeds 55; Sunflower seeds 60; Peas 45; Chickpeas 45; Tofu 65; Walnuts 50 and Wheat 60.

BEELZEBUB BUBBLE AND SQUEAK

One of Mark Twain's eleven cats was called Beelzebub, solely because he wanted his children to learn how to pronounce a difficult word.

1 small potato
2.4 oz (70g) cooked soya beans
   or 4.3 oz (120g) tofu
   or 0.7 oz (20g) TVP (Textured Vegetable Protein)
   or 1.8 oz (50g) soya sprouts
2 teaspoons oil
2 teaspoons yeast powder
1 tablespoon grated vegetable
$\frac{7}{8}$ teaspoon Vegekit powder

Cook the potato. Mash the choice of soya products. Add remaining ingredients and mix thoroughly into a firm dough-like texture.

Protein 27.9 per cent, Fat 14.9 per cent, Ash 7.6 per cent

PICKLED PROSE

'The cat was odd in other ways; when her master was at his desk writing, she would always select a small piece of writing paper on which she sat down, no doubt putting herself on a literary footing with him. Her diet was also extraordinary; she would eat pickles and drink brandy-and-water.'

Fruit Between the Leaves
by Andrew Wynter

(5 days' food)
11.5 oz (325g) cooked chick peas
   or 5.1 oz (145g) uncooked chick peas
2.2 oz (66g) TVP (Textured Vegetable Protein)
   or 7.2 oz (202g) firm tofu
2.2 oz (66g) yeast powder
0.7 fl oz (24ml) oil
½ teaspoon salt
   or 2 teaspoons soya sauce
1½ tablespoons Vegekit powder
Seasoning e.g. garlic powder, onion powder, etc.

If using uncooked chick peas, soak in water until doubled in size (usually overnight). Drain, cover with fresh water and cook until tender. Drain thoroughly and crush. Add remaining ingredients and mix thoroughly.

Protein 31.7 per cent, Fat 12.4 per cent, Mg 0.17 per cent

MONTY'S MORSEL

Monty, named after General Montgomery of Alamein, was the ginger cat that belonged to Derek and Jeannie Tangye.

'And when our guests arrived, a hundred or more packing the cottage, a cacophony of laughter and talk, cigarette smoke clouding the rooms, people sitting on the floor and the stairs, glasses everywhere, Jeannie and I rushing around with bottles and plates of cold food, Monty was as cool as a cucumber. He would stroll from room to room, pausing beside a guest when the praise was high, even deigning to jump on a lap, ignoring the cat haters, refusing with well-bred disgust any morsel dangled before him by some well-meaning admirer.'

'A Cat in the Window', *The World of Forever*
by Derek Tangye

2.3 oz (65g) cooked rice
3.2 oz (90g) cooked soya beans
   or 5.6 oz (160g) tofu
   or 0.9 oz (26g) TVP (Textured Vegetable Protein)
   or 2.4 oz (65g) soya sprouts
1 tablespoon oil
2 teaspoons yeast powder
$\frac{1}{2}$ teaspoon Vegecat powder
$\frac{1}{3}$ teaspoon soya sauce

If using TVP, gently hydrate by simmering in hot water until tender and drain. Mix all ingredients together thoroughly into a firm dough-like texture.

Protein 29.4 per cent, Fat 20.5 per cent, Ash 6.1 per cent, Mg 0.17 per cent

111

A WEALTH OF PEAS

I

'The Owl and the Pussy-cat went to sea
In a beautiful pea-green boat,
They took some honey, and plenty of money,
Wrapped up in a five-pound note.
The Owl looked up to the stars above,
And sang to a small guitar,
"O lovely Pussy! O Pussy, my love,
What a beautiful Pussy you are,
You are,
You are!
What a beautiful Pussy you are!"'

'The Owl and the Pussy-Cat'
The Complete Nonsense of Edward Lear
edited by Holbrook Jackson

2.7 oz (75g) cooked or sprouted chickpeas
1½ tablespoons yeast powder
1 tablespoon oil
½ teaspoon Vegecat powder
⅓ teaspoon soya sauce

Mix all ingredients thoroughly into a firm dough-like texture.

Protein 28.9 per cent, Fat 21.4 per cent, Ash 5.5 per cent, Mg 0.15 per cent

DIDDLETY, DIDDLETY DUMPLING

'Pussy cat ate the dumplings,
Pussy cat ate the dumplings,
    Mamma stood by,
    And cried, Oh, fie!
Why did you eat the dumplings?

Traditional Nursery Rhyme

1.1 oz (30g) maize meal (corn meal)
   or 4.2 oz (120g) whole maize
1.7 oz (50g) cooked soya beans
   or 3.0 oz (85g) tofu
   or 0.5 oz (15g) TVP (Textured Vegetable Protein)
   or 1.3 oz (35g) soya sprouts
1 tablespoon oil
1 tablespoon yeast powder
$\frac{1}{2}$ teaspoon Vegecat powder
$\frac{1}{3}$ teaspoon soya sauce

If using TVP, gently hydrate by simmering in hot water until tender and drain. Mix all ingredients together thoroughly into a firm dough-like texture.

Protein 23.8 per cent, Fat 21.2 per cent, Ash 5 per cent, Mg 0.15 per cent

GALLOPING GOURMET

'Oh I am a cat that likes to
Gallop about doing good
So
One day when I was
Galloping about doing good, I saw
A Figure in the path; I said:
Get off! (Be-
cause
I am a cat that likes to
Gallop about doing good)
But he did not move, instead
He raised his hand as if
To land me a cuff
So I made to dodge so as to
Prevent him bringing it orf,
Un-for-tune-ately I slid
On a banana skin
Some Ass had left instead
Of putting in the bin.'

'The Galloping Cat',
The Collected Poems of Stevie Smith

Rice Lentil Soya

1.2 oz (35g) cooked rice
1.2 oz (35g) cooked soya beans
   or 2.2 oz (60g) tofu
   or 0.4 oz (10g) TVP (Textured Vegetable Protein)
   or 0.9 oz (25g) soya sprouts
1.5 oz (45g) cooked or sprouted lentils
1 tablespoon oil
1½ tablespoons yeast powder
½ teaspoon Vegecat powder
⅓ teaspoon soya sauce

If using TVP, gently hydrate by simmering in hot water until tender and drain. Mix all ingredients together thoroughly into a firm dough-like texture.

Protein 29 per cent, Fat 20.4 per cent, Ash 6 per cent, Mg 0.14 per cent

Oat Soya

2.5 oz (70g) cooked soya beans
    or 4.5 oz (130g) tofu
    or 0.7 oz (20g) TVP (Textured Vegetable Protein)
    or 1.9 oz (55g) soya sprouts
0.6 oz (17g) flaked oats
    or 3.1 oz (90g) cooked oats
    or 2.1 oz (35g) prepared bulghur
    or 1 slice wholemeal bread
1 tablespoon oil
1 tablespoon yeast powder
$\frac{1}{2}$ teaspoon Vegecat powder
$\frac{1}{3}$ teaspoon soya sauce

If using TVP, gently hydrate by simmering in hot water until tender and drain. If using flaked oats gently hydrate by adding a small quantity of hot water. Mix all ingredients together thoroughly into a firm dough-like texture.

Protein 31.2 per cent, Fat 26.1 per cent, Ash 5.7 per cent, Mg 0.19 per cent

The recipes in this section are used by kind permission of the Vegan Society.

DRINK OR TREAT

'You own a dog but you feed a cat.'

Jenny De Vries

pollyanna pickering

116

MILKY MEW

'Pussy-cat Mew jumped over a coal,
And in her best petticoat burnt a great hole.
Pussy-cat Mew shall have no more milk
Till she has mended her gown of silk.'

Traditional Nursery Rhyme

8 fl oz (230ml/1 cup) goats' milk
1 tablespoon oatbran and oatgerm

Blend the milk with the oatbran and wheatgerm.

POUSSIE PALACE PUNCH

'Poussie, poussie, baudrons,
Whaur hae ye been?'
'I've been tae London
Tae see the Queen.'

'Poussie, poussie, baudrons,
Whit gat ye there?'
'I gat a guid fat mousikie,
Rinnin' up a stair!'

'Poussie, poussie, baudrons,
Whit did ye dae wi' it?'
'I pit it in ma meal-poke,
Tae eat tae ma breid.'

Traditional Old Scottish Nursery Rhyme

2½ fl oz (75m1/⅓ cup) cranberry juice
5¼ fl oz (150/⅔ cup) water *

Mix the cranberry juice with the water.

* It is best to use filtered or bottled water. The mineral content in tap water varies from region to region and the water supply in many areas is treated with chemicals. If you do purchase bottled water, make sure it has been purified by a natural method and check the contents. Choose a brand with the lowest possible amount of chlorides, nitrates and sodium. Too much sodium is bad for animals with a heart condition or diabetes and can also lead to hypertension. If you haven't already studied a typical analysis of bottled water, you will be amazed at the differences between the various brands:

	Chloride	Nitrate	Sodium
Ballygowan	28.0	9.0	15.0
Buxton	42.0	0.1	24.0
Caledonian	8.0	2.0	6.8
Chiltern Hills	15.0	5.0	8.0
Evian	4.5	3.8	5.0
Highland Spring	7.5	1.0	6.0
Strathmore	125.0	5.0	46.0
Vittel	–	0.6	7.3
Volvic	8.4	6.3	9.4
Welsh Mineral Water	12.0	1.3	5.0

Some plastic bottles can have an adverse effect on health, so whenever possible buy water in glass bottles. This has the added advantage that they can be recycled.

SNOWDROP MILK

In Lewis Carroll's *Through the Looking-Glass. And What Alice Found There*, Alice is angry at the mischief that Kitty has been doing and says:

'I'm going to tell you all your faults. Number one: you squeaked twice while Dinah was washing your face this morning... Number two: you pulled Snowdrop away by the tail just as I had put down the saucer of milk before her! What, you were thirsty, were you? How do you know she wasn't thirsty too? Now for number three: you unwound every bit of the worsted while I wasn't looking!'

3¾ oz (110g/¾ cup) coley or cod fillet
12 fl oz (340ml/1½ cups) goats' milk
a pinch of mint, chopped

Put the coley or cod, goats' milk and mint in a saucepan. Bring to the boil and then simmer for 12 minutes. Drain, retaining the liquid – Snowdrop Milk. Allow to cool before serving. Use the coley for a meal, adding a little vegetable and brown rice or make some Musical Memory Bites (page 123)

Yields: approx. 5¼ fl oz/150ml

BODGER'S RICE PUDDING

Richard Surman, a true ailurophile and the author of *Cathedral Cats*, recalls in his Introduction a favourite family feline:

'Bodger, the grandest and most regal tabby of the house, was a glutton. We found him one night, ankle deep in the middle of a large dish of rice pudding, eating it as fast as he could.'

2 oz (55g/just over ¼ cup) lamb and mutton mince, boiled
a pinch of rosemary
1¼ oz (35g/¼ cup) pudding rice
10 fl oz (285ml/1¼ cups) goats' milk

Put the mince, rosemary, rice and goats' milk in a greased casserole dish. Cover and bake at 300°F for 2 hours.

Yields: approx. 8½ oz/240g

TAFFY TOPAZ TAPIOCA

'Taffy, the topaz-coloured cat,
Thinks now of this and now of that,
But briefly of his meals.
Asparagus, and cream, and fish,
Are objects of his Freudian wish;
What you don't give, he steals.

'Taffy Topaz' by Christopher Morley
Cats – A Celebration in Words and Paintings
selected by Helen Exley

2 oz (55g/⅓ cup) tapioca
10 fl oz (285ml/1¼ cups) Snowdrop Milk (page 120)
2 tablespoons filtered water
¼ teaspoon organic catnip
½ teaspoon honey

In a saucepan soak the tapioca in the Snowdrop Milk and filtered
water for 1 hour. Place over a low heat and simmer for 1 hour. Add
the catnip and honey.

Yields: approx. 7¾ oz/225g

Note: Catnip is not suitable for kittens.

MUSICAL MEMORY BITES

Cat owners often feel guilty about leaving their pets alone for hours on end. Peter Neville, the feline behaviour therapist, brought out a video called *Cool For Cats* with the sole purpose of keeping a cat 'amused and occupied in the comfort of his own living room while his owners are away'.

Edith Sitwell, the English poet, bought a record entitled 'Baby Don't Be Blue' specially for her cat, Leo, while she was living in Paris. One imagines her putting on this song as she tried to sneak out of the door surreptiously in the hope that it would ease Leo's disappointment when he realised she had left.

So, if you are going out leaving your cat alone and don't want to feel guilty just put on your cat's favourite CD or video with a plate of Musical Memory Bites which your cat can munch at his leisure. My niece, Kristin Kemnitzer, tells me that her cats, Dusty Whiskers and Checkers, particularly like Ravel's *L'Enfant et Les Sortilèges*, a magical opera based on a story by Sidonie-Gabrielle Colette. At the end of Scene I is the renowned cat duet sung in cat language – 'Le Chat et La Chatte' – in which the Black Cat serenades the White Cat in the moonlit garden.

2½ oz (75g/½ cup) coley or cod fillet, poached in goats' milk and flaked

1½ oz (45g/just under ¼ cup) tinned pilchards in tomato sauce, drained and mashed

4½ oz (125g/1 cup) organic wholemeal flour

4½ oz (125g/just under 1 cup) cornmeal

1 teaspoon dried mint

2 fl oz (55ml/¼ cup) Fish Brew (page 84)

1 tablespoon unrefined grapeseed oil

2 free range eggs, beaten

Mix all the ingredients together. Roll out on a floured surface, approximately $\frac{1}{8}''$–$\frac{1}{4}''$ thickness. Make into various shapes – bird, fish, etc. using small pastry cutters. Place the bites on a greased baking tray and bake in the oven at 360°F for 15–20 minutes. Break up and serve.

Yields: approx. 36 bites

NIBBLES FOR RAINING CATS & DOGS

There has always been an underlying distinction between the characters of cats and dogs and I think the following anonymous quote from *The Quotable Cat* compiled by C. E. Crimmins illustrates the basic difference between them perfectly:

'If I tell my dog, "Come here," he runs right over with a "Yes, what can I do for you?" look. The cat's response is "Put it in writing, and I'll get back to you."'

5 oz (140g/just over 1 cup) Shipton Mill sunflower and wheat flour
1½ oz (45g/¼ cup) ground rice
1 oz (30g/¼ cup) carob powder
¼ teaspoon brewers' yeast
1 tablespoon extra virgin olive oil
1 large free range egg, beaten
1½ fl oz (45ml/just under ¼ cup) goats' milk
2 tablespoons filtered water

Mix all the ingredients together. Drop heaped teaspoons of the mixture onto a greased baking tray. Bake in the oven at 360°F for 20 minutes. Your cat may prefer these broken up.

Yields: approx. 30 nibbles

RECIPES FOR AILING CATS

'Any cat who misses a mouse pretends it was aiming for the dead leaf.'

Charlotte Gray

FOOD FOR LIFE

The strange tale *The Jealous One* by Giles Gordon takes place at a reception for the newly-weds Edward and Angela. Champagne is flowing, the cake has been cut and:

'The cat was almost sick, would have been had Edward not forgotten to feed him that morning, before he left the house in such a rush amidst so much clatter and turmoil. The beginning of the end, the first time in four years he'd forgotten to feed him.'

Suddenly a gunshot is heard. Edward has been shot dead and the cat is the one holding the smoking revolver... The moral of this story could be: Don't forget to feed the cat.

9 oz (255g/1¼ cups) low-fat chicken mince
7 fl oz (200ml/just under 1 cup) Meaty Brew – made with chicken bones (page 84)
1½ oz (45g/⅓ cup) cooked brown rice
½ teaspoon multi-vitamin/mineral powder

Boil the chicken mince in the Meaty Brew for 25 minutes. Add the brown rice and multi-vitamin/mineral powder.

Yields: approx. 10 oz/285g

This is a good basic, easily digested meal for most cats needing a bit of 'TLC'. It is also simple to make, so there is no excuse for not feeding the cat!

GYP CHICKEN

'I had a nefarious old cat, Gyp, who used to open the cupboard door and eat any biscuits accessible. Gyp had a stroke of paralysis, and believed he was going to die. He was in a fright: Mr Horace Hutchinson observed him and said that this cat justly entertained the most Calvinistic apprehensions of his future reward. Gyp was nursed back into health, as was proved when we found him on the roof of an outhouse with a cold chicken in his possession. Nothing could be more human.'

Andrew Lang

1 fresh chicken breast fillet (6 oz/185g)
1 teaspoon extra virgin olive oil
a sprinkling of fresh garlic
1 oz (30g/½ cup) curly kale, finely chopped and cooked
1½ oz (45g/⅓ cup) cooked brown rice
1 tablespoon live goats' yoghurt
¼ teaspoon lecithin granules
½ Vitamin E tablet (25iu), crushed
½ Vitamin C tablet 250–500mg (depending on the size of cat) crushed

Place the chicken breast on a roasting rack. Cover the chicken with the olive oil and sprinkle with garlic. Bake in the oven for 45 minutes at 375°F. Chop the chicken into small pieces and mix with the curly kale, brown rice and live goats' yoghurt. Add the lecithin granules, Vitamin E and C tablets once the meal has been cooked and cooled down a bit – heat destroys the vitamins.

Yields: approx. 8 oz/230g

BUTLER'S CHOICE

Samuel Butler's sister wanted him to have a Persian cat, but he had other ideas and wrote to her from 15 Clifford's Inn, London EC on 21 October 1885, saying:

'No, I will not have any Persian cat; it is undertaking too much responsibility... I have already selected a dirty little drunken wretch of a kitten to be successor to my poor old cat. I don't suppose it drinks anything stronger than milk and water but then, you know, so much milk and water must be bad for a kitten that age – at any rate it looks as if it drank; but it gives me the impression of being affectionate, intelligent, and fond of mice, and I believe, if it had a home, it would become more respectable; at any rate I will see how it works.'

Samuel Butler, Author of Erewhon (1835–1902) : A Memoir
Vol. II, 1885–1916
by Henry Festing Jones

1 chicken breast (4½ oz/120g), cut up into small pieces
12 fl oz (340ml/1½ cups) filtered water
a pinch of basil, chopped
2 oz (55g/just under ½ cup) sweet potato, peeled and diced
½ oz (15g/⅛ cup) frozen peas
feline anti-oxidant supplement

Put all the ingredients, except the feline supplement, in a saucepan. Bring to the boil and simmer for 20–25 minutes. Give the feline supplement according to the instructions on the label.

Yields: approx. 6 oz/170g

A NOSE FOR FOOD

'The Cat, who was suffering from indigestion and feeling seriously indisposed, could only eat thirty-five mullet with tomato sauce, and four portions of tripe with Parmesan cheese; and because she thought the tripe was not seasoned enough she asked three times for the butter and grated cheese.'

from *Pinocchio*
by Carlo Collodi

3 oz (85g/just under $\frac{1}{2}$ cup) raw rabbit, cut up
1 tablespoon tomato ketchup
$\frac{1}{2}$ teaspoon goats' yoghurt
$\frac{1}{2}$ oz (15g/$\frac{1}{4}$ cup) broccoli florets, finely chopped
feline multi-vitamin/mineral supplement

Mix together the rabbit, tomato ketchup, yoghurt and broccoli. Add the feline supplement according to the instructions on the label.

Yields: approx. $4\frac{1}{4}$ oz/125g

Raw fresh food is universally recommended for pets with cancer.

GAVROCHE GOULASH

Among Théophile Gautier's collection of cats described in *The White and Black Dynasties*, we find the black cat, Gavroche (named after the character in Victor Hugo's novel, *Les Misérables*):

'Sometimes in his [Gavroche's] truant wanderings he picked up emaciated comrades, lean with hunger, and brought them to his plate of food to give them a treat in his good-natured, lordly way. The poor creatures, with ears laid back and watchful side-glances, in fear of being interrupted in their free meal by the broom of the housemaid, swallowed double, triple, and quadruple mouthfuls, and ... they licked the plate as clean as if it had been washed and polished by one of Gerard Dow's or Mieris's Dutch housewives.'

3 oz (85g/just under ½ cup) raw organic lamb and mutton mince
5 oz (140g/1¼ cups) cooked brown rice
feline anti-oxidant supplement

Mix together the lamb and mutton mince and brown rice. Give the feline supplement according to the instructions on the label.

Yields: approx. 8 oz/230g

DAME TROT'S BROTH

'Dame Trot came home one wintry night
A shivering starving soul,
But Puss had made a blazing fire
And nicely trussed a fowl.
Next morning Puss got up betimes,
The breakfast cloth she laid;
And, ere the village clock struck VIII,
The tea and toast she made.'

Traditional Nursery Rhyme

8 fl oz (230ml/1 cup) filtered water
1 teaspoon Bovril
a clove cooked garlic, diced
a small piece of dry toast (organic bread)
feline anti-oxidant supplement

Heat the water. Add the Bovril and garlic. Allow to cool before serving with the toast. Give the feline supplement according to the instructions on the label.

Pollyanna Pickering

CONCLUSION

We are all becoming more aware of the need to eat healthily and it is a logical conclusion to extend that philosophy to our cats as well.

I am no longer content to feed my cats with cheap tins or cans of unspecified content and find as they get older they need a purer diet to keep them in optimum health. Having so many cats, I need to avoid vets' bills as much as possible and find that with proper nutrition, herbs, homoeopathy and vitamin supplements in the majority of cases I can help my cats live to a ripe old age with very little veterinary intervention. (I would of course let them have drugs or surgery if it were necessary.) However, for me the proof is in the pudding and with the help of alternative remedies I have had some marvellous results with very sick cats who could not be helped by conventional medicine.

As my own homoeopathic doctor said to me, 'If you put the right petrol in your car it runs perfectly and if you put the right food into people or animals they too will function properly.' Unfortunately that still doesn't take into account the modern world of pollution, chemicals, hormones and antibiotics, but with the help of anti-oxidants, vitamins, minerals, essential oils, homoeopathy, herbs, pure foods and tender loving care we can at least help to counteract their harmful effects.

Alexandra Bastedo

FOOD AND ITS VITAMIN AND MINERAL CONTENT

(correlated by Pet Nutrition Concepts)

Carbohydrates

Whole grains, syrup, honey, fruits and vegetables.

Fats

Butter, margarine, vegetable oils, fats in meat, whole milk and milk products, nuts (except peanuts) and seeds.

Proteins

Meats, fish, poultry, free range eggs, whole milk and milk products, soybean products and whole grains.

Vitamin A

Liver, free range eggs, yellow fruits and vegetables, dark green fruits and vegetables, whole milk and milk products.

Vitamin B-1

Brewers' yeast, whole grains, blackstrap molasses, organ meats, free range egg yolks, legumes and nuts (except peanuts).

Vitamin B-2

Brewers' yeast, whole grains, blackstrap molasses, organ meats, free range egg yolks, legumes and nuts (except peanuts).

Vitamin B-6

Meats and organ meats, brewers' yeast, whole grains, blackstrap molasses, wheatgerm, legumes and green leafy vegetables.

Vitamin B-12

Organ meats, fish, free range eggs, cheese, whole milk and milk products.

Biotin

Free range egg yolks, liver, unpolished rice, brewers' yeast, whole grains, sardines and legumes.

Choline

Free range egg yolks, organ meats, brewers' yeast, wheat germ, soybeans, fish and legumes.

Folic Acid

Dark green leafy vegetables, organ meats, brewers' yeast, root vegetables, whole grains, oysters, salmon, and whole milk.

Inositol

Whole grains, citrus fruits, brewers' yeast, molasses, meat, whole milk, nuts (except peanuts), and vegetables.

Niacin

Lean meats, poultry, fish brewers' yeast, rice bran, whole milk and milk products.

Para Amino Benzoic Acid (PABA)

Organ meats, wheat germ, yoghurt, molasses and green leafy vegetables.

Pangamic Acid

Brewers' yeast, rare steaks, brown rice, sunflower, pumpkin and sesame seeds.

Pantothenic Acid

Organ meats, brewers' yeast, egg yolks, legumes, whole grains, wheat germ and salmon.

Vitamin C

Citrus fruits, rose hips, acerola cherries, alfalfa seeds, sprouts, cantaloupe, strawberries, broccoli, tomatoes and green peppers.

Vitamin D

Salmon, sardines, herring, vitamin D-fortified milk and milk products, free range egg yolks and organ meats.

Vitamin E

Cold pressed oils, eggs, wheat germ, organ meats, molasses, sweet potatoes and leafy vegetables.

Vitamin K

Green leafy vegetables, free range egg yolks, safflower oil, blackstrap molasses, cauliflower and soybeans.

Bioflavanoids

Citrus fruits, fruits, blackcurrants and buckwheat.

Unsaturated Fatty Acids

Vegetable oils and sunflower seeds.

Calcium

Whole milk and milk products, green leafy vegetables, shellfish and molasses.

Chromium

Honey, grapes, raisins, corn oil, whole grain cereals and brewers' yeast.

Cobalt

Organ meat, poultry, whole milk, green leafy vegetables and fruits.

Copper

Organ meats, seafood, nuts (except peanuts), legumes, molasses and raisins.

Iodine

Seafood and kelp.

Iron

Organ meats and meats, eggs, fish, poultry, blackstrap molasses, green leafy vegetables and dried fruits.

Magnesium

Seafood, whole grains, dark green vegetables, molasses and nuts (except peanuts).

Manganese

Whole grains, green leafy vegetables, legumes, nuts (except peanuts), pineapples and egg yolks.

Molybdenum

Legumes, whole grain cereals, whole milk, kidney, liver and dark green vegetables.

Phosphorus

Fish, meats, poultry, eggs, legumes, whole milk and milk products, nuts (except peanuts) and whole grain cereals.

Potassium

Lean meats, whole grains, vegetables, dried fruits, legumes and sunflower seeds.

Sodium

Seafood, celery, processed foods and whole milk products.

Sulphur

Fish, garlic, onions, eggs, meats, cabbage and brussels sprouts.

Zinc

Pumpkin and sunflower seeds, seafood, organ meats and meats, mushrooms, brewers' yeast, soybeans, herring, eggs and wheat germ.

VITAMINS, MINERALS, ANTI-OXIDANTS AND ESSENTIAL OILS

Acidophilus

Maintains a favourable micro-floral balance in the gastro-intestinal tract and may assist the natural digestive processes. Recommended for cats on long term antibiotics and steroid medication.

Alfalfa (Medicago sativa)

Native to Europe, Asia and North Africa. Nutritive herb with a high vitamin and mineral content.

Aloe Vera

Native to Africa, aloe has been traditionally used both externally and internally for first aid and skin conditions and as a protective and healing agent in gastro-intestinal conditions. Also possesses laxative, anti-inflammatory and anti-oxidant properties.

Bilberry

Native to Europe and North America, bilberry's high anthocyanin content gives it anti-oxidant properties and is known to increase capillary blood circulation, with overall benefits for the eyes and cardiovascular system.

Bioflavanoids

Also known as flavanoids, bioflavanoids are colourful anti-oxidants found in plants. Aid absorption of vitamin C and in maintaining the integrity of blood vessels and normal circulation.

Biotin

Involved in energy release from food, carbohydrate and protein metabolism. Required for normal growth and development of bone marrow, fur, skin and muscle.

Boron

Research suggests it may play a role in maintaining healthy, strong bones. Also needed for absorption of calcium.

Betaine

Found in beetroot. Betaine is an intermediate in the conversion of choline to glycine, and helps to break down fats.

Calcium

Works in the body with magnesium and vitamin D and maintains healthy bones and teeth. Helps in the function of nerves and muscles and has a role in the utilisation of amino acids.

Cat's Claw

Traditionally used by the Indians as a powerful immune system booster, anti-flammatory muscle-relaxant and for its beneficial cardiovascular effects.

Celery

Native to European countries, celery is a good cleansing and diuretic herb.

Cellulase

An enzyme that breaks down cellulose, used to aid digestion of vegetable matter and fibrous foods.

Chlorella

Green micro-algae, rich in chlorophyll, suggested for the immune system, and detoxifies the liver, blood and bowel from chemicals and heavy metals.

Chondroitin

It plays an essential role in the formation of joint cartilage.

Chromium

Essential mineral involved in regulating blood sugar levels and carbohydrate, fat, protein and cholesterol metabolism.

Cod Liver Oil

Source of omega-3 EFAs (EPA and DHA) as well as vitamins A and D, which maintains normal growth, supple joints and healthy fur and skin.

Co-enzyme Q10

Essential mineral for energy production in all cells, notably those of the heart, muscle tissue, brain and liver. Powerful anti-oxidant and important for the immune system and healthy gums.

Collagen

Collagen is a low molecular weight protein, consisting of a series of amino-acids. It is a building block of bone cartilage, and is responsible for the framework and shape of connective tissue.

Colloidal Minerals

Microscopic particles found in ecologically preserved areas which are easily absorbed by the gut and may contribute to optimum nutrition.

Copper

Required for red blood cell formation and involved in several enzyme systems. Helps utilise iron, and aids development of bone, brain and nerve tissue.

Cranberry

Known to restore a healthy acid balance in the urinary tract, also has anti-bacterial properties.

Dandelion

Dandelion grows wild in most parts of the world and is known for its powerful and safe diuretic properties. It is an effective detoxifying herb.

Devil's Claw

This African plant derives its name from the appearance of its tough, barbed fruit. It is used traditionally for inflammation and swelling in arthritic conditions.

Echinacea

Native to North America, known to possess anti-bacterial and anti-viral activity, and is useful in strengthening the immune system.

Evening Primrose Oil

Rich source of gamma-linolenic acid (GLA) and linoleic acid (LA), which are poly-unsaturated essential fatty acids (EFAs). These are involved in regulating the nervous, cardiovascular and reproductive systems, skin conditions and other biological functions.

Feverfew

Originally from south-eastern Europe, feverfew is known to possess analgesic properties. It also has anti-inflammatory properties and reduces body temperature.

Folic Acid

Important for formation of red blood cells, ensuring a healthy nervous system and RNA/DNA development. Also has a role in protein metabolism and prevents anaemia.

Garlic

Originally from central Asia, garlic is now grown world-wide. Benefits the digestive and immune systems and assists in maintaining a healthy heart, circulation and normal cholesterol levels. Also known to display anti-bacterial, anti-fungal and anti-viral properties.

Glucosamine

For healthy joint care.

Iodine

Utilised by the thyroid gland to produce hormones which help regulate the metabolism.

Iron

Required in formation of haemoglobin. Oxygen carrier throughout the body and important for muscle function. Prevents anaemia.

Juniper Berry

Juniper has been traditionally used in Europe, Asia and North America for its antiseptic properties, commonly for urinary tract infections.

Lecithin

An emulsifier of fats, lecithin is a source of many nutrients, notably phosphatidyl choline which is involved in biological functions in cell membranes, cardiovascular and nervous systems and the mechanisms that store and transport fats and cholesterol.

Leucine

An amino acid involved in stress, energy and muscle metabolism.

Liquorice Root

Native to south-eastern Europe and south-western Asia, known traditionally for its powerful anti-inflammatory, demulcent and expectorant properties. It is particularly useful for inflammatory conditions of the digestive system and joints.

Lysine

An amino acid involved in energy production, regulating calcium absorption, collagen production, neurotransmitter and other amino acid production.

Magnesium

Constituent of skeletal structure and teeth. Role as a co-factor for energy production. Vital for nerve transmission, muscles and a proper heart beat. Required for absorption of calcium and potassium. Cats need only a very small amount of magnesium.

Manganese

Co-factor for many body enzymes. Responsible for various functions such as synthesis of bone/cartilage, superoxide dismutase (SOD helps prevents tissue damage due to free radicals), protein synthesis and energy production.

Meadowsweet

Native to Europe, meadowsweet contains anti-inflammatory, astringent and diuretic properties.

Methionine

An amino acid involved in the production of other sulphur amino acids.

Omega 3 EFAs

EPA is believed to have anti-inflammatory properties, healing to maintain healthy joints and cardiovascular system. DHA is thought to play an important part in the transmission of electrical impulses to the brain.

Phosphorus

Important role in skeletal structure. Required for nerve and muscle function.

Potassium

Important for nerve transmission, maintaining normal heart rate and as an electrolyte to ensure correct fluid balance and healthy muscle function.

Propolis

Known to possess anti-oxidant and anti-bacterial activities and used as an immune system enhancer.

Protease

Protein digesting enzyme.

Pumpkin Seed

A popular medicinal plant in the Americas, the seeds are rich in EFAs which have anti-inflammatory effects.

Rose Hips

Natural source of vitamin C and bioflavanoids.

Rutin

Bioflavanoid found in buckwheat.

Silica

Rich in glycosaminoglycans which are components of bone, cartilage and arterial tissue. They are also involved in maintaining normal regulation of the heart, brain and peripheral circulation.

Skullcap

A native North American herb, known as a nerve tonic, it helps to support and nourish the nervous system and calms and relieves stress and anxiety.

Spirulina

One of nature's original wholefoods, it grows as a dark plankton in the oceans of the world, serving as a basic link in the food chain. One of the richest sources of highly digestible proteins, this algae also contains vitamins, minerals, enzymes and other nutrients e.g. linoleic acids, vitamin B12, vitamin E, amino acids, iron, RNA, DNA and chlorophyll. Aids the immune system.

Starflower/Borage Oil

Mixture of mainly mono- and poly-unsaturated oils, which has approximately 50 per cent more GLA than an equivalent dose of evening primrose oil.

St. John's Wort

Native to Europe, herbalists have long used it as a tonic for anxiety. It also has anti-viral, anti-spasmodic and astringent properties.

Taurine

A sulphur amino acid that is the most abundant amino acid in the heart and the second most in the brain. It has neurotransmitter functions and regulates sodium, calcium and potassium levels in cell membranes It also has anti-oxidant activity. Cats die without taurine in their diet.

Uva Ursi

Native to Europe, known as one of the best natural urinary antiseptic and diuretic, may be beneficial in urinary tract infections.

Valerian

Native to Europe and northern Asia, valerian has been used to treat anxiety and nervous irritability since at least Roman times. Has muscle relaxant properties.

Vitamin A

Important for healthy eyes, skin, fur, bones, teeth and mucous membranes of the respiratory, digestive and urinary tracts.

Vitamin B 1

Important for the release of energy from food, maintaining the integrity of the nervous system and several other metabolic functions. It is also needed for normal appetite and growth.

Vitamin B 2 (Riboflavin)

Involved in energy release from food. Helps maintain healthy skin, fur, eyes and lining of the nose and throat. Role also in formation of liver enzymes and normal functioning of mental and muscular systems.

Vitamin B 3 (Niacin or nicotinic acid)

Energy release from food. Essential for proper function of mental, nervous and digestive systems. Role in formation of red blood cells and steroids, is needed for healthy circulation.

Vitamin B 5 (Pantothenic acid)

Energy release from food. Essential for function of brain, immune system and healthy skin. Considered by many as an 'anti-stress' vitamin. Required for antibody formation, wound healing and growth.

Vitamin B 6 (Pyridoxine)

Energy release from food. Important for fat and amino acid metabolism. Required for production of red blood cells and maintenance of fluid balance and healthy nervous system and brain function.

Vitamin B 12 (Cyanocobalamin)

Bone marrow and red blood cell regeneration. DNA synthesis and healthy nervous system.

Vitamin B Complex

Group of 'B' vitamins necessary for proper function of the nervous system and healthy maintenance of skin, hair, eyes, intestinal muscles and liver.

Vitamin C

Necessary for maintenance of collagen, bones, gums, teeth and blood capillaries. Aids iron absorption and utilisation of folic acid. Anti-oxidant properties, protects against damage to vitamins A and E. Involved in cell/tissue repair. Role in formation of red blood cells and adrenal gland hormones. Helps to maintain the immune system and normal cholesterol levels.

Vitamin D

Required for absorption of calcium and phosphorus to maintain healthy bones, teeth, skin, heart, nerves and thyroid.

Vitamin E

Powerful anti-oxidant, prevents oxidation of certain fats and vitamins. Helps to maintain normal blood clotting and red blood cell integrity. Plays an important role in maintaining healthy function of the cardiovascular and reproductive systems and healthy skin condition.

Vitamin K

Essential for blood clotting and plays a role in the maintenance of healthy bones.

Zinc

Key role in maintenance of nervous, reproductive and immune systems. Required for sensation of taste and smell. Integral part of insulin and required for blood sugar levels. Role in certain enzyme catalysis. Helps wound healing, normal growth, good vision and maintenance of healthy skin.

CONVERSION TABLES

Liquid Measurements

Imperial	Recommended ml
1 fl oz	30 ml
2 fl oz	55 ml
3 fl oz	85 ml
4 fl oz ($\frac{1}{4}$ pint USA)	115 ml
5 fl oz ($\frac{1}{4}$ pint UK)	140 ml
6 fl oz	170 ml
7 fl oz	200 ml
8 fl oz ($\frac{1}{2}$ pint USA)	230 ml
9 fl oz	255 ml
10 fl oz ($\frac{1}{2}$ pint UK)	285 ml
11 fl oz	315 ml
12 fl oz	340 ml
13 fl oz	370 ml
14 fl oz	400 ml
15 fl oz	430 ml
16 fl oz (1 pint USA)	455 ml
17 fl oz	485 ml
18 fl oz	515 ml
19 fl oz	540 ml
20 fl oz (1 pint UK)	570 ml

Solid Measurements

Imperial	Recommended g
1 oz	30 g
2 oz	55 g
3 oz	85 g
4 oz ($\frac{1}{4}$ pound)	115 g
5 oz	140 g
6 oz	170 g
7 oz	200 g
8 oz ($\frac{1}{2}$ pound)	230 g
9 oz	255 g
10 oz	285 g
11 oz	315 g
12 oz ($\frac{3}{4}$ pound)	340 g
13 oz	370 g
14 oz	400 g
15 oz	430 g
16 oz (1 pound)	455 g

1 kilogram (kg) equals 2.2 lbs

Useful Equivalents

1.76 UK pints	= 1 litre
2 USA pints	= 1 quart
4 USA quarts	= 1 gallon
1 UK cup	= 10 fl oz
1 USA cup	= 8 fl oz

N.B. The cups referred to in the recipes are USA cups.

Measuring Spoons

(approximate universal conversion)

$\frac{1}{4}$ teaspoon	= 1.25 ml
$\frac{1}{2}$ teaspoon	= 2.5 ml
1 teaspoon	= 5 ml
1 tablespoon	= 15 ml

Useful Measurements

3 mm	$= \frac{1}{8}''$
6 mm	$= \frac{1}{4}''$
1 cm	$= \frac{1}{2}''$
2 cm	$= \frac{3}{4}''$
2.5 cm	$= 1''$
5 cm	$= 2''$

Oven Temperatures

C	F	Gas Mark
70	150	
80	175	
100	200	
110	225	$\frac{1}{4}$
120	250	$\frac{1}{2}$
140	275	1
150	300	2
160	325	3
180	350	4
190	375	5
200	400	6
220	425	7
230	450	8
240	475	9
260	500	
270	525	
290	550	

OTHER PREFERRED PRODUCTS

AND WHERE TO FIND THEM...

The following are products which have been recommended by cat lovers:

Acorn Supplements Ltd
PO Box 103
Robertsbridge
East Sussex TN32 5ZT
Tel: 01580 881333
Fax: 01580 811444

(Homoeopathic, aromatherapy, Bach Flower Remedies and natural healing products for cats)

Ainsworths Homoeopathic Pharmacy
36 New Cavendish Street
London W1M 7LH
Tel: 0171 935 5330
Fax: 0171 486 4313

Animal Actives
11 Southgate Road
Potters Bar
Hertfordshire EN6 5DR
Tel/Fax: 01707 646948

(Natural pet products for positive pet health – slippery elm complex, canidor, euphrasia, echinacea)

Animal Fair
17 Abingdon Road
Kensington High Street
London W8 6AH
Tel: 0171 937 0011

(One of the best pet shops in London; major stockists of most products)

Biggles
66 Marylebone Lane
London W1M 5FF
Tel: 0171 224 5937
Fax: 0171 935 8454

(Finest special recipe sausages – 85 per cent meat, including lamb and mint, lamb and rosemary, chicken and tarragon sausages.)

Bones Dog & Catalogue
The Upper Mill
Coln St Aldwyns
Cirencester
Gloucestershire GL7 5AJ
Tel: 01285 750 007
Fax: 01285 750 100

(Their catalogue includes flea patrol bandanna, flea patrol bandanna oil, non-spill water bowl, pets' picnic box, etc.)

Chlorella Products Ltd
The Stables, Upper Farm
Hinton Parva, Swindon
Wiltshire SN4 0DH
Tel: 01793 791111
Fax: 01793 791122

(Chlorella, Chlorella Growth Factor, KDF/GAC water filters)

Comfy Pet & People Products
2–4 Parsonage Street
Bradninch, Nr. Exeter
Devon EX5 4NW
Tel: 01392 881285
Fax: 01392 881188

Freshlands
196 Old Street
London EC1V 9FR
Tel/Fax: 0171 490 3170

(Organic foods and natural remedies)

Fur Feather & Fins
54 Elm Grove
Southsea
Hampshire PO5 lJG
Tel: 01705 862935
Fax: 01705 817742

(Stockists of multiple pet products)

Green Ark Animal Nutrition
Unit 7B, Lineholme Mill
Burney Road, Todmorden
West Yorkshire OL14 6HX
Tel/Fax: 01706 812188

(Herbal tonic, garlic powder, and many other products)

Harrods Ltd
Pet Shop
Brompton Road, Knightsbridge
London SW1X 7XL
Tel: 0171 730 1234
Fax: 0171 581 0470

Helios Homoeopathics Ltd
89–95 Camden Road
Tunbridge Wells
Kent TN1 2QR
Tel: 01892 515111/511555
Fax: 01892 515116

(The Veterinary Homoeopathy Basic Kit plus individual range)

Johnson's Veterinary Products Ltd.
5 Reddicap Trading Estate
Sutton Coldfield
West Midlands B75 7DF
Tel: 0121 378 1684
Fax: 0121 311 1758

(List of products include Coal tar and sulphur shampoo and Tea tree shampoo, citrus flea repellent and herbal flea collar)

Natural Friends
PO Box 103 Robertsbridge
East Sussex TN32 5ZT
Tel: 01580 881222
Fax: 01580 881444

(Suppliers of flora herbal products, Bach Flower Remedies, aromatherapy oils, homoeopathic Nelsons products, homoeopathic books, pet memorials, Acorn anal clear, herbal de-wormers, flea collars and flea clear herbal capsules)

Nelson Homoeopathic Pharmacy
73 Duke Street
London W1M 5DH
Tel: 0171 629 3113
Tel: 0171 495 2404 (Mail Order)
Fax: 0171 495 0013

Alexandra's Pet Nutrition Concepts Ltd.
PO Box 201
Chichester
West Sussex PO20 7YT
Tel: 07071 223266

Pet Pavilion
Chelsea Farmers Market
125 Sydney Street
London SW3 6NR
Tel: 0171 376 8800

(Stockists of multiple pet products)

Pets Corner
Country Garden Centre
Bognor Road, Merston
Chichester
West Sussex PO20 6EG
Tel: 01243 530606

(Stockists of multiple pet products – ring 0990 329818 for addresses of other branches in the south of England)

PETsMART
Tel: 0990 114499
(Ring for your nearest store - stockists of multiple pet products)

Pure Multi-Nutrients
8 Victory Place
Crystal Palace
London SE19 3RW
Tel/Fax: 0181 771 4522

(Organic foods and natural remedies – mail order)

Revital Health Shop
35 High Road
London NW10 2TE
Tel: 0181 459 3382
Fax: 0181 459 3722

(Mail order – a major stockist of various homoeopathic products)

SPR
Poultry & Smallholder Centre
Greenfields Farm, Fontwell Avenue
Eastergate, West Sussex PO20 6RU
Tel: 01243 542815
Fax: 01243 544662

(Cat foods and various feline products)

Shipton Mill
Long Newnton
Tetbury
Gloucestershire GL8 8RP
Tel: 01666 505050
Fax: 01666 504666

(Various range of organic flours, oats etc. – mail order)

Sloane Health Shop
32 Sloane Square
London SW1W 8AQ
Tel: 0171 730 7046
Fax: 0171 823 5521

(Mail order throughout the world – various homoeopathic & bio-chemical remedies, Corpore Sano anti-parasite shampoo and tonic)

Stock Nutrition
Station Road, Yaxham
Norfolk NR19 1RD
Tel: 01362 694957
Fax: 01362 699067
(Genie – bio-degradable disinfectant, Protest – for digestive problems, Moor Gold – holistic tonic for older and nervous cats and kittens, Dyna-Mite – 'herbal insect repellent for fleas and Dyna-Mite shampoo. These products are also available through SPR – address above.)

Thermal Concepts Ltd.
Parc Teifi Business Park
Cardigan SA43 1EW
Tel: 01239 614005
Fax: 01239 615191

(Snuffle Safe – microwave heatpad)

Treasurecots Pet Beds
Salters Lane, Lower Moor
Worcestershire WR10 2PE
Tel: 01386 860144
Fax: 01386 861427

(Hygienic, non-allergic, draughtproof comfortable cat beds)

The Vegan Society
Donald Watson House
7 Battle Road
St Leonards-on-Sea
East Sussex TN37 7AA
Tel: 01424 427393
Fax: 01424 717064

(Vegecat and Vegekit – animal-free supplements)

The Watermill
Little Saikeld, Penrith
Cumbria CA10 1NN
Tel: 01768 881523

(Organic stoneground flours and other organic produce – family-run business with the philosophy 'care for the planet, for sustainable energy and agriculture, for the health of the soil, plants and animals' – mail order catalogue available)

Weald & Downland Open Air Museum
Singleton, Chichester
West Sussex PO18 0EU
Tel: 01243 811363
Fax: 01243 811475

(Singleton stoneground wholemeal flour)

Wellington Vet Pharmacy
39 Knightsbridge
London SW1X 7NL
Tel: 0171 235 5621
Fax: 0171 235 0158
(The only veterinary pharmacy inside the M25. They stock Nelsons and Weleda homoeopathic products – mail order throughout the world)

APPROPRIATE ADDRESSES

Advocates for Animals
10 Queensferry Street
Edinburgh EH2 4PG
Scotland
Tel: 0131 225 6039

(The Protection of Animals
from Cruelty. The Prevention of
the Infliction of Suffering. The
Abolition of Vivisection.)

**Agricultural and Veterinary
Group of the The Royal
Pharmaceutical Society of
Great Britain (RPSGB)**
1 Lambeth High Street
London SE1 7JN
Tel: 0171 735 9141
Fax: 0171 735 7629

**The American Cat Association
Inc.**
Susie Page, Secretary
8101 Katherine Avenue
Panorama City
California 91402
USA
Tel: 00 1 818 781 5656
Fax: 00 1 818 781 5340

**American Cat Fanciers
Association, Inc. (ACFA)**
PO Box 203, Point Lookout
Missouri 65726 USA
Tel: 00 1 417 334 5430
Fax: 00 1 417 334 5540

(Contact for the Atlantic RIM:
Mr Tony Morace,
406 Orange St., Springfield,
MA 01108
Tel: 00 1 413 733 3387)

Animal Aid
The Old Chapel
Bradford St
Tonbridge
Kent TN9 lAW
Tel: 01732 364546
Fax: 01732 366533

(Against all animal abuse)

Animal Aunts
Smugglers Cottage
Green Lane, Rogate
Petersfield
Hampshire GU31 5DA
Tel: 01730 821529
Fax: 01730 821057

(A nationwide service providing house and animal sitters)

Animal Health Trust
PO Box 5
Newmarket
Suffolk CB8 8JH
Tel: 01638 661111
Fax: 01638 665789

Animal Medical Centre
Veterinary Treatment and
Diagnostic Centre
242 Cricklewood Lane
London NW2 2PU
Tel: 0181 450 2228
Fax: 0181 208 1382

The Association of Chartered Physiotherapists in Animal Therapy (ACPAT)
Morland House
Salters Lane
Winchester
Hampshire SO22 5JP
Tel: 01962 844390

Association of Pet Behaviour Counsellors (APBC)
PO Box 46
Worcester WR8 9YS
Tel/Fax: 01386 751151

The Blue Cross
Shilton Road
Burford
Oxfordshire OX18 4PF
Tel: 01993 822651
Fax: 01993 823083
(Caring for sick animals, re-

homing stray and abandoned pets)

The British Allergy Foundation
Deepdene House
30 Bellegrove Road
Welling
Kent DA16 3PY
Tel: 0181 303 8525
Fax: 0181 303 8792

British Association of Homoeopathic Veterinary Surgeons
Alternative Veterinary
Medicine Centre
Chinham House
Stanford-in-the-Vale
Faringdon
Oxfordshire SN7 8NQ
Tel: 01367 710324
Fax: 01367 718243

(Information and list of homoeopathetic vets)

British Homoeopathic Association
27a Devonshire Street
London W1N 1RJ
Tel: 0171 935 2163

The British Small Animal Veterinary Association (BSAVA)
Kingsley House, Church Lane
Shurdington, Cheltenham
Gloucestershire GL51 5TQ
Tel: 01242 862994

British Union for the Abolition of Vivisection (BUAV)
16a Crane Grove
London N7 8LB
Tel: 0171 700 4888
Fax: 0171 700 0252

The British Veterinary Association (BVA)
7 Mansfield Street
London W1M 0AT
Tel: 0171 636 6541
Fax: 0171 436 2970

Capital Cats Inc.
Ms G Mitchell, Secretary
PO Box 404
Dickson, ACT 2602
Australia
Tel: 00 61 6 231 6538/263 4630

The Cat Association of Britain
Mill House, Letcombe Regis
Oxfordshire OX12 9JD
Tel: 01235 766543

(The British Member of The Federation Internationale Feline)

Cat and Rabbit Rescue Centre
Holborow Lodge,
Chalder Lane
Sidlesham, Chichester
West Sussex PO20 7RJ
Tel: 01243 641409

(Monique Turk, Nigel Oddy and Helen Luff)

Cat and Rabbit Rescue Centre
Feralands, Roudham Road
East Harling,
Norfolk NR16 2QN
Tel: 01953 718529

(Judi Mapplebeck)

Cat Owners Association of Western Australia Inc.
Mrs Pam Parish, Registrar
PO Box 135
Claremont, WA 6010
Australia
Tel: 00 61 9 384 2500

The Cat Welfare Liaison Group
Secretary: Mrs Harrington
79 Pilgrims' Way
Kemsing, Sevenoaks
Kent TN15 6TD
Tel: 01732 761689

The Cats Protection League
17 Kings Road
Horsham
West Sussex RH13 5PN
Tel: 01403 221900
Helpline: 01403 221927
Fax: 01403 218414

Celia Hammond Animal Trust
High Street, Wadhurst
East Sussex TN5 6AG
Tel: 01892 783820/783367
Fax: 01892 784882

(Inexpensive neutering clinics and animal rescue)

Children in Hospital and Animal Therapy Association (CHATA)
87 Longland Drive, Totteridge
London N20 8HN
Tel/Fax: 0181 445 7883

The Cinnamon Trust
Foundry House
Foundry Square
Hayle, Cornwall TR27 4HH
Tel: 01736 757900
Fax: 01736 757010

(Helps to keep the elderly and physically weak with their pets)

Compassion in World Farming (CWF)
Charles House
5A Charles Street
Petersfield
Hampshire GU32 3EH
Tel: 01730 264208/268863
Fax: 01730 260791

Co-ordinating Cat Council of Australia (CCCA)
Mrs Val Stewart, Secretary
1461 Healesville-Kooweerup
Road, Woori Yallock, VIC 3139
Australia
Tel: 00 61 3 59 646 808
Fax: 00 61 3 59 615 538

Council of Federated Cat Clubs
of Queensland Inc.
Ms Marie Mahoney, Secretary
497 Oakey Flat Road
Morayfield, Queensland 4506

Australia
Tel: 00 61 7 5498 6078
Fax: 00 61 7 5497 9385

Country Fairs
Woodend
Slindon Bottom Road
Fontwell, Arundel
West Sussex BN18 0SL
Tel: 01243 544181
Mobile: 0831 430608
Fax: 01243 544068

Whightwick Mill
Bridgenorth Road
Whightwick, Wolverhampton
Staffordshire WV6 0XX
Tel: 01902 765053
Mobile: 0850 896637
Fax: 01902 765052

The Dogs' Home Battersea (Cat Section)
4 Battersea Park Road
London SW8 4AA
Tel: 0171 622 3626
Fax: 0171 622 6451

The Federation Internationale Feline (FIFe)
Little Dene, Lenham Heath
Maidstone, Kent ME17 2BS
Tel: 01622 858510
Fax: 01622 850908

Feline Advisory Bureau (FAB)
PO Box 6
Tisbury
Wiltshire SP3 6TE
Tel: 01747 871872
Fax: 01747 871873

Feline Association of South Australia
Mrs A Noonan, Registrar
10 Paxton Court
Redwood Park, SA 5097
Australia
Tel: 00 61 8 381 6470

Friends of the Earth Trust
26–28 Underwood Street
London N1 7JQ
Tel: 0171 490 1555
Fax: 0171 490 0881

The Governing Council of the Cat Fancy (GCCF)
4–6 Penel Orlieu
Bridgwater
Somerset TA6 3PG
Tel: 01278 427575

Governing Council of the Cat Fancy of Australia and Victoria
PO Box 242
Mitcham, Victoria 3122
Australia

Hand To Paw – Animal Rescue Directory
North Cottage
Great Hayes
Headley Common Road
Headley
Surrey KT18 6NE
Tel: 01372 375302/0831 619847
Fax: 01372 375302

The Homoeopathy Society
2 Powis Place

Great Ormond Street
London WC1N 3HT
Tel: 0171 837 9469
Fax: 0171 278 7900

Institute of Trading Standards Administration
35 Hadleigh Business Centre
351 London Road
Hadleigh, Essex SS7 2BT
Tel: 01702 559922
Fax: 01702 559902

The International Cat Association (TICA)
PO Box 2684
Harlingen, Texas 78551
USA
Tel: 00 1 210 428 8046

Meat and Livestock Commission
Snowdon Drive
Winterhill,
Milton Keynes
Buckinghamshire
MK6 1AX
Tel: 01908 677577
Fax: 01908 609221

Ministry of Agriculture, Fisheries and Food (MAFF)
Ergon House,
c/o Nobel House
17 Smith Square,
London
SW1P 3JR
Tel: 0171 270 8080
Helpline: 0645 335577

Ministry of Agriculture, Fisheries and Food (MAFF)
Government Buildings
(Toby Jug Site)
Hook Rise South
Tolworth, Surbiton
Surrey KT6 7NF
Tel: 0181 330 4411
Fax: 0181 337 3640

(List of quarantine kennels)

National Animal Welfare Trust (NAWT)
Tyler's Way
Watford by-pass
Watford
Hertfordshire WD2 8HQ
Tel: 0181 950 8215/0177
Fax: 0181 420 4454

The National Anti-Vivisection Society Limited
261 Goldhawk Road
London W12 9PE
Tel: 0181 846 9777
Fax: 0181 846 9712

(Animal Defenders, The Lord Dowding Fund for Humane Research)

National Office of Animal Health Limited (NOAH)
3 Crossfield Chambers
Gladbeck Way, Enfield
Middlesex EN2 7HF
Tel: 0181 367 3131
Fax: 0181 363 1155

The National Pet Register
Thorpe Underwood Hall
York YO5 9SZ
Tel: 0700 0800 123

(Computerised tracing for lost cats – registration and insurance)

National Pet Week
PO Box 101
Northwood
Middlesex HA6 3RH
Tel/Fax: 0181 428 7369

(People for Pets – Pets for People)

New Zealand Cat Fancy Club Inc. (NZCF)
National Secretary, Chris McNeil
PO Box 12096
Ahuriri, Napier
New Zealand

Passports for Pets
20 Seymour Road
London SW18 5JA
Tel: 0181 870 5960
Fax: 0181 870 9223

(The alternative to quarantine)

People for the Ethical Treatment of Animals (PETA)
PO Box 3169
London NWl 2JF
Tel: 0181 785 3113

People's Dispensary For Sick Animals (PDSA)
Whitechapel Way
Priorslee, Telford
Shropshire TF2 9PQ
Tel: 01952 290999
Fax: 01952 291035

Pet Advisory Committee (PAC)
1 Dean's Yard, Westminster
London SW1P 3NR
Tel: 0171 340 2211
Fax: 0171 976 8276

(Providing information and advice on pets in society to Parliament, and national and local government)

Pet Care Trust
Bedford Business Centre
170 Mile Road
Bedford MK42 9YZ
Tel: 01234 273933
Fax: 01234 273550

The Pet Food Manufacturers' Association (PFMA)
Suite 12, 12–13 Henrietta Street
London WC2E 8LH
Tel: 0171 379 9009
Fax: 0171 379 8008/3898

Pet Fostering Service Scotland (PFSS)
PO Box 6, Callander FK17 8ZU
Scotland
Tel: 01877 331496

(Provides volunteers to give short-term care for pets belonging to elderly people)

Pet Health Council
Thistledown Cottage
49 Main Street
Sewstern,
Grantham
Lincolnshire NG33 5RF
Tel: 01476 861379
Fax: 01476 861336

The Protesters Animal Information Network Limited (P.A.I.N.)
The Lodge, Broadhurst Manor
Horsted Keynes
West Sussex RH17 7BG
Tel: 01342 811377
Fax: 01342 811213

(Carla Lane and Celia Hammond. Carla Lane has also set up the excellent charity Animal Line and Animal Rescue. A caring organization for animal welfare.)

Queensland Independent Cat Council Inc.
Mrs Chris Taylor, Secretary
34 Mitchell Street
Barellan Point,
Queensland 4306
Australia
Tel: 00 61 7 3294 6248

Raystede Centre for Animal Welfare Limited
Raystede,
Ringmer
East Sussex BN8 5AJ
Tel: 01825 840252

Royal College of Veterinary Surgeons
Belgravia House
62–64 Horseferry Road
London SW1P 2AF
Tel: 0171 222 2001
Fax: 0171 222 2004

Royal Society for the Prevention of Cruelty to Animals – (RSPCA)
Causeway, Horsham
West Sussex RH12 1HG
Tel: 01403 264181
Fax: 01403 241048
Cruelty Line: 0990 555999

Royal Veterinary College
Camden Campus
Royal College Street
London NW1 0TU
Tel: 0171 468 5000
Fax: 0171 388 2342

(The Beaumont Animals' Hospital – Tel: 0171 387 8134)

Hawkshead Campus
Hawkshead Lane,
North Mimms
Hatfield, Herts. AL9 7TA
Tel: 01707 666333
Fax: 01707 652090

(ACT – Animal Care Trust)

The St Andrew Animal Fund
10 Queensferry Street
Edinburgh EH2 4PG
Scotland
Tel: 0131 225 2116
Fax: 0131 220 6377

(To promote humane attitudes towards animal life and the development of a proper understanding and appreciation of all living things)

Scottish Society for the Prevention of Cruelty to Animals (SPCA)
Braehead Mains
603 Queensferry Road
Edinburgh EH4 6EA
Tel: 0131 339 0222
Fax: 0131 339 4777

Shirrin Persian and Pedigree Longhair Rescue
Mallams, Broad Oak
Sturminster Newton
Dorset DT10 2HD
Tel/Fax: 01258 472073

(Jenny Parkhouse)

Society for Companion Animal Studies (SCAS)
10b Leny Road
Callander
Scotland FK17 8BA
Tel/Fax: 01877 330996

(Includes Pet Loss Advisory Group)

Soil Association
86 Colston Street
Bristol BS1 5BB
Tel: 0117 929 0661
Fax: 0117 925 2504
(Directory of organic farm shops and box schemes)

**Ulster Society for the
Prevention of Cruelty
to Animals (USPCA)**
Unit 4, Boucher Business
Centre, Apollo Road
Belfast BT12 6HP
Tel: 01232 660479
Fax: 01232 381911
Animal Helpline: 0990 134329

**Universities Federation For
Animal Welfare**
8 Hamilton Close,
South Mimms
Potters Bar
Herts. EN6 3QD
Tel: 01707 658202
Fax: 01707 649279

Vegan Society
Donald Watson House
7 Battle Road
St Leonards-on-Sea
East Sussex TN37 7AA
Tel: 01424 427393
Fax: 01424 717064

Vegetarian Society
Parkdale, Dunham Road

Altrincham
Cheshire WA14 4QG
Tel: 0161 928 0793
Fax: 0161 926 9182

Which?
PO Box 44
Hertford X SG14 1SH
Tel: 01992 822800
Fax: 0171 8308585

The Willow Cattery
2nd Avenue, Almodington
Chichester
West Sussex PO20 7LF
Tel: 01243 511411

(Terry and Jan Ditcham – a
particularly good, very
hygienic, caring cattery which
will do different menus for
pernickety cats.)

**World Society for the
Protection of Animals**
2 Langley Lane
London SW8 1TJ
Tel: 0171 793 0540
Fax: 0171 793 0208

NOTABLE NAMES

Mr Trevor Adams BVSc CertBR VetMFHom MRCVS
The Orchard Veterinary Surgery
King Street, Glastonbury
Somerset BA6 9JX
Tel: 01458 832972

(Homoeopathic vet)

Mr Richard Allport BVetMed VetMFHom MRCVS
Natural Medicine Veterinary Centre
11 Southgate Road, Potters Bar
Hertfordshire EN6 5DR
Tel: 01701 662058
Fax: 01701 646948

(Referral service in: acupuncture, Bach flower therapy, electro crystal therapy, homoeopathy, healing, herbal medicine, aromatherapy, physiotherapy, massage, osteopathy and behaviour counselling; promotes a large range of natural products (*see* Animal Actives in Preferred Products)

Dr Ian Billinghurst
PO Box 703
Lithgow
New South Wales 2790
Australia

(Noted Australian vet)

Katie Boyle
J. Gurnett Ltd
2 New Kings Road, London SW6 4SA
Tel: 0171 736 7828

(Patron of Animal Health Trust and Animal Welfare Trust)

Mr Peter Brown BVSc MRCVS IVAS Certified
Kingley Veterinary Centre
Oldwick Farm, West Stoke Road
Lavant, Nr Chichester
West Sussex PO18 9AA
Tel: 01243 528899
Fax: 01243 528877

(Veterinary surgeon and acupuncturist)

Mr Keith Butt MA VetMB MRCVS
8 Kynance Mews
Gloucester Road
London SW7 4QP
Tel: 0171 584 2019

(A London general vet whose particular interests are skin and cancer.)

Mr John Carter BVetMed MRCVS
290 Kenton Road
Harrow, Middlesex HA3 8DD
Tel: 0181 907 6051

(A London general vet who specialises in cancer and leukaemia. Good success rates.)

Mr Timothy Couzens BVetMed VetMFHom MRCVS
Holistic Veterinary Medicine Centre
The Village Works, London Road
East Hoathly, Lewes
East Sussex BN8 6QA
Tel: 01825 840966

(Homoeopathic vet, acupuncturist and author of homoeopathic books, referral service for holistic veterinary medicine.)

Paddy Cutts
25 Hollies Road
Ealing, London W5 4UU
Tel: 0181 568 4960

(Animal photographer and author of cat books)

Mr Christopher Day MA VetME VetMFHom MRCVS
Alternative Veterinary Medicine Centre
Chinham House, Stanford-in-the-Vale
Faringdon
Oxfordshire SN7 8NQ
Tel: 01367 710324

(Homoeopathic vet)

Juliette de Bairacli Levy
(Extremely knowledgeable on herbs and homoeopathy and nutrition for cats. Writer of *The Complete Herbal Handbook For the Dog and Cat.*)

Mr Mark Elliott BVSc VetMFHom MRCVS
Kingley Veterinary Centre
Oldwick Farm, West Stoke Road
Lavant, Nr Chichester
West Sussex PO18 9AA
Tel: 01243 528899
Fax: 01243 528877

(Our homoeopathic vet and adviser and author of homoeopathic books)

Dr Bruce Fogle DVM(Gu) MRCVS
86 York Street
London W1H 1DP
Tel: 0171 723 2068
(Excellent vet, journalist and writer of superb books on animals)

Mr Peter Graham Goodrich BVetMed VetMFHom MRCVS
Kingston House
85 Main Street
Pembroke, Dyfed SA71 4DB
Tel: 01646 622943

(Homoeopathic vet)

Mr Peter Gregory BVSc VetMFHom MRCVS
6 Queen Street
Newcastle under Lyme
Staffordshire ST5 lED
Tel: 01782 719771

(Homoeopathic vet)

Celia Hammond
High Street, Wadhurst
East Sussex TN5 6AG
Tel: 01892 783820/783367
Fax: 01892 784882

(Founder of animal rescue centres and inexpensive neutering and spaying clinics for cats and dogs)

Mr John Hoare BVSc VetMFHom MRCVS
12 Martins Road
Hanham, Bristol
Avon BS15 3EW
Tel: 0117 967 7067

(Homoeopathic vet)

Mr Francis Hunter VetMFHom MRCVS
Arun Veterinary Group
121 Lower Street
Pulborough
West Sussex RH20 2BP
Tel: 01798 872089
Fax: 01798 872080

(Homoeopathic vet, author – Chairman of the British Homoeopathic Association)

Mrs Barbara Jones BVMS VetMFHom MRCVS
Oakwood Veterinary Centre
Babbinswood Farm
Whittington, Oswestry
Shropshire SY11 4PH
Tel: 01691 679699

(Homoeopathic vet & feline acupuncturist)

Mr Richard Lockyer BVM&S VetMFHom MRCVS
Highfield Veterinary Surgery
White Stubbs Lane
Broxbourne
Hertfordshire EN10 7QA
Tel: 01992 440738

(Homoeopathic vet)

Mr Tom Lonsdale BVetMed MRCVS
Riverstone Veterinary Hospital
Garfield Road, Riverstone
New South Wales 2765
Australia

Dr Richard H Pitcairn, DVM, PhD
Director
1283 Lincoln Street
Eugene, Oregon 97401
USA
Tel: 00 1 503 342 7665

(co-author of *Dr Pitcairn's Complete Guide to Natural Health for Dogs and Cats*)

Mr John Saxton BVetMed VetMFHom MRCVS
Tower Wood Veterinary Group
27 Tinshill Road
Leeds LS16 7DR
Tel: 01132 678419

(Homoeopathic vet)

Miss Christine Shields BVSc VetMFHom MRCVS
43 Main Street
Warton, Carnforth
Lancashire LA5 9NT
Tel: 01524 736765

(Homoeopathic vet)

William George Smith
29 Elm Road
Westergate, Chichester
West Sussex PO20 6RQ
Tel: 01243 543991

(Spiritual healer – animals and humans)

Mrs June Third-Carter BVMS VetMFHom MRCVS
Hillhead House
Lonmay, By Fraserburgh
Aberdeenshire AB43 4UP
Tel: 01346 532948

(Homoeopathic vet)

Mrs Susan Thomas MA VetMB VetMFHom MRCVS
Tower Wood Veterinary Group
27 Tinshill Road
Leeds LS16 7DR
Tel: 01132 678419

(Homoeopathic vet)

BIBLIOGRAPHY

CAT CARE

The Cat Care Question and Answer Book
Barry Bush BVSc PhD FRCVS
Bloomsbury, 1986

Cats: Homoeopathic Remedies
George McLeod MRCVS DVSM
The C. W. Daniel Company, 1990

Cat Sense – Inside the Feline Mind
Akif Pirincci and Rolf Degen
translated from the German by Anthea Bell
Fourth Estate, 1994

Catwatching – The Essential Guide To Cat Behaviour
Desmond Morris
Jonathan Cape, 1986

Claws and Purrs Understanding the Two Sides of Your Cat
Dr Peter Neville
Sidgwick & Jackson, 1992

The Complete Cat Book
Paddy Cutts
Ultimate Editions, 1995

The Complete Herbal Handbook for the Dog and Cat
Juliette de Bairacli Levy
Faber and Faber, 1992

Do Cats Need Shrinks?
Dr Peter Neville
Pan, 1993

Homoeopathy for a Healthier Cat
Mark Elliot BVSc, VetMFHom, MRCVS and Tony Pinkus Bpharm, MRPPharmS, 1998

Let's Cook For Our Cat
Edmund R Dorosz BSA DVM
Our Pet's Inc., 1995

My Cat is Driving Me Crazy!
Grace McHatty and Tim Couzens BVetMed VetMFHom MRCVS
Robinson, 1995

Natural Healing for Dogs & Cats
Diane Stein
The Crossing Press, 1993

*The Natural Remedy Book for
Dogs & Cats*
Diane Stein
The Crossing Press, 1994

*The New Natural Cat
A Guide for Caring Owners*
Anitra Frazier with Norma
Eckroate
Aurum Press, 1996

*101 Essential Tips: Caring for
Your Cat*
Andrew Edney & David Taylor
Dorling Kindersley, 1995

People are Pets
Francis Hunter MRCVS
VetMFHom and Steven Kayne
PhD MRPharm
S DAgVetpharm MPS(NZ)
LFHom (Pharm)
British Homoeopathic
Association, 1997

*Dr Pitcairn's Complete Guide to
Natural Health for Dogs & Cats*
Richard H. Pitcairn DVM PhD
and Susan Hubble
Pitcairn MS
Rodale Press Inc., 1995

*Small Animal Clinical Nutrition
III*
Lon D. Lewis, Mark L. Morris,
Jr., Michael S. Hand
Mark Morris Associates

Vegetarian Cats & Dogs
James A. Peden
Harbingers of a New Age, 1995

*The Well Cat Book
The Classic Comprehensive
Handbook of Cat Care*
Terri McGinnis DVM
Random House, 1993

You & Your Cat
David Taylor BVMS FRCVS
Dorling Kindersley, 1986

*Feline Fact and Fiction
Alice's Adventures in Wonderland
And Through the Looking-Glass,
And What Alice Found There*
Lewis Carroll
Macmillan, 1984

The Book of Cats
Edited by George MacBeth &
Martin Booth
Bloodaxe, 1992

Captain's All
W. W. Jacobs
Hodder & Stoughton, 1905

Cathedral Cats
Richard Surman
Fount, 1997

Cats
A Celebration in Words and Paintings
selected by Helen Exley
Exley, 1992

Cats in Books
A Celebration of Cat Illustration through the Ages
Selected and introduced by Rodney Dale
The British Library, 1997

The Church Cat
Clerical Cats in Stories and Verse
edited by Mark Bryant
Hodder & Stoughton, 1997

The Collected Poems of Stevie Smith
Allen Lane, 1975

Collected Stories for Children
Walter de la Mare
Faber and Faber, 1970

The Complete Nonsense of Edward Lear
edited and introduced by Holbrook Jackson
Faber and Faber

The Complete Poems
John Keats
edited by John Barnard
Penguin, 1988

The Europe That Was
Geoffrey Household
Michael Joseph, 1979

The Faber Book of Favourite Fairy Tales
edited by Sara and Stephen Corrin
Faber and Faber, 1988

A Gentleman Publisher's Commonplace Book
John G. Murray
John Murray, 1996

The Literary Companion to Cats
Clare Boylan
Sinclair-Stevenson, 1995

Magnus The Orkney Cat
Kathleen Russell
Words by Marion Campbell
A Paul Harris book for
Canongate Press, 1993

My Wilderness Wildcats
Mike Tomkies
Macdonald and Jane's, 1977

Opera & Operetta
Michael White & Elaine Henderson
HarperCollins, 1997

The Oxford Nursery Rhyme Book
assembled by Iona and Peter Opie
Oxford University Press, 1979

Pinocchio – The Tale of a Puppet
Carlo Collodi
The original translation by
M.A. Murray revised by
G. Tassinari
J.M. Dent & Sons, 1973

The Quotable Cat
A Collection of Quotes, Facts, and
Lore for Feline Fanciers
selected and compiled by
C.E. Crimmins
Running Press, 1992

Quotable Cats
The Quintessential Collection
of Feline Wisdom
Running Press, 1977

Samuel Butler, Author of Erewhon
(1835–1902):
A Memoir by Henry Festing
Jones Vol. II 1885–1916
Macmillan, 1919

Shelley Poetical Works
edited by Thomas Hutchinson
Oxford University Press, 1967

Vivien – The Life of Vivien Leigh
Alexander Walker
Orion

Wiliam Shakespeare
The Complete Works
Oxford University Press, 1994

The World of Forever
A Memorial Anthology of
Quotations From the Minack
Chronicles
Derek Tangye
Michael Joseph, 1997

LITERARY ACKNOWLEDGEMENTS

Acknowledgement and thanks are due to the following for kindly giving permission to reproduce or make reference to copyright material:

Canongate Books Ltd. (14 High Street, Edinburgh EHl ITE, Scotland): extract from *Magnus the Orkney Cat* by Kathleen Russell and Marion Campbell. © copyright Kathleen Russell 1993.

Edmund R. Dorosz, BSA DVM: extracts and recipes from *Let's Cook For Our Cat*, Our Pet's Inc., distributed in the UK by Abbeywood Publishing.

A. M. Heath on behalf of the estate of Geoffrey Household: extract from 'Abner of the Porch', *The Europe That Was*, published by Michael Joseph, 1979.

James MacGibbon (11 Wentworth Mansions, Keats Grove, London NW3 2RL): extract from 'The Galloping Cat', *The Collected Poems of Stevie Smith*, published by Allen Lane, 1975.

John Murray (Publishers) Ltd.: extract from *A Gentleman Publisher's Commonplace Book* by John G. Murray, 1996. © This selection: John R. Murray 1996.

The Orion Publishing Group Ltd.: extract from *Vivien - The Life of Vivien Leigh* by Alexander Walker, published by Weidenfeld and Nicolson; extract from *Pinocchio* by Carlo Collodi, published by J.M. Dent.

By permission of Oxford University Press: extract from 'Verses on a Cat', *Shelley Poetical Works*, edited by Thomas Hutchinson, 1967.

Penguin Books Ltd.: extract from 'A Cat in the Window', *The World of Forever*, A Memorial Anthology of Quotations From the Minack Chronicles by Derek Tangye, published by Michael Joseph Ltd., 1997. Individual passages copyright © the Estate of Derek Tangye: A Cat in the Window 1962.

The Society of Authors as the literary representative of the Estate of W. W. Jacobs: extract from 'The White Cat' , *Captain's All*, published by Hodder & Stoughton, 1905.

Richard Surman: extracts from *Cathedral Cats*, published by Fount (an imprint of HarperCollins Publishers), 1997. Copyright © 1993 Richard Surman.

Mike Tomkies: extract from *My Wilderness Wild Cats*, published by Macdonald and Jane's, 1977. Copyright © pictures, text and appendix by Mike Tomkies 1977.

ALEXANDRA'S CATS

At the start of the book I had twenty-seven cats and kittens, by the end I had only fifteen as twelve had been re-homed. I have now been taking in cats in need and re-homing them for seventeen years and it has been excruciatingly difficult to part with any of them. However cats are individuals and need lots of love and individual attention so of the hundreds that have passed through my hands the majority are better off with the many kind people who have taken them on rather than being part of a large colony.

My own permanent cats that I refer to in the book are:

Rexy, the black Cornish Rex aged seventeen.

Abbie, the black and white Rex-Abyssinian cross aged seventeen.

Blackie, the black moggie, aged seventeen.

Cardy, the white Cornish Rex aged fourteen.

Snowdrop, the white ex-feral moggie who lived behind the dustbins and is cured of cancer aged ten.

Coco, the brown and white Cornish Rex aged ten.

Caramel, the brown and white Cornish Rex aged eight.

Toffee, the Rex-Siamese aged eight.

Camilla, the grey Rex-Chinchilla aged fourteen.

Sheba, the lilac-point Siamese aged ten.

Byron, the British Short-Haired Tip aged ten.

Alfie, the tabby and white long-hair aged seven months.

Duchess, the white moggie aged eighteen months.

Duke, Duchess' white son, aged seven months.

Baron, Duchess' tabby son of seven months.

Deceased are:

Hodge, my beautiful grey, blue-eyed Tonkinese who died aged sixteen although he was diagnosed with Feline Aids at six.

Coley, my lovely white and black moggie who died of kidney failure – he was a dried biscuit addict and lived until the age of thirteen.

Whitey, my white third cat who was run over and killed on our lethal country lane aged five.

Missing is Kim, my first incredible cat, a black half-Burmese. He would now be nineteen.

JEANNIE'S FASTIDIOUS FELINES

Family, friends and neighbours were most obliging in allowing their fastidious felines to sample my recipes in this book. I even had volunteers from overseas... I would just like to extend my sincere and grateful thanks to all the owners for their enthusiasm and for being so conscientious in keeping records of their cats' likes and dislikes. Not to sound trite, but truly without these cats this book would not have been possible:

United Kingdom

Gingerbread Banfield
Little Wee Banfield
Tiger Tim Banfield
Charlie Banks
Leo Boutwood
Max Boutwood
Harry de Bruyn
Cashew Cole
Misty Cole
Teabag Cole
Amy Deveries
Bagheera Eden
Barnaby Edward
Daisy Edwards
Jess Elliott
Kizzy Finch
Curtley Ambrose Flind
John Flind

Caspar Gomersall
Figgy Gomersall
Jenny Heyes
Lizzie Heyes
Hattie Hope
Leo Hope
Purrdi Hope
Graham Joyner
Kristel Knight
Lucky Knight
Berry Lockwood
Billo Lockwood
Katy Lockwood
Rosie Lockwood
Sophie Lockwood
Sulu Lockwood
Sunny Lockwood
Yogi Lockwood
Luis Mooney
Rosie Naylor
Basil Robertson
Wiggy Robertson
Paddy Rogerson
Patty Rogerson
Angus Shepherd
Millie Shepherd
Spike Shepherd
Arfur Smith
Bobby Snow
Crunchy Snow
Tigger Snow
Charlie Spence
Rocky Spence
Rusty Spence
Solly Spence
Gnasher Surman
Nipper Surman
George Kit Vaughan
Cosmic Winterflood

Australia

Where's Wally Sirett

France

Penny Burnett
Francesca Cladel

New Zealand

Ariel Brodie
Smokie Newland
Mr Flinty McSquinty
Benson Horatio Ross

Spain

Tuly Martin
Simon Templar

United States of America

Checkers Kemnitzer
Dusty Whiskers Kemnitzer

Pollyanna Pickering

Pollyanna Pickering is recognised as one of Europe's foremost wildlife artists. She studied at Rotherham Art School and the London Central School of Art, and has been working freelance since 1969. Her work has been reproduced as fine art and limited edition prints, as well as on greeting cards, calendars and other giftware. Many charities have commissioned her work, including Guide Dogs for the Blind and WSPA.

For 15 years she ran a registered bird hospital, caring for and re-releasing injured and orphaned birds of prey, as well as other wildlife.

'I have always maintained that whether a black cat crossing your path is lucky or unlucky depends on whether you are a man or a mouse.'

Bernard Levin
from *A Gentleman Publisher's Commonplace Book*
by John G. Murray